Art For The Soul

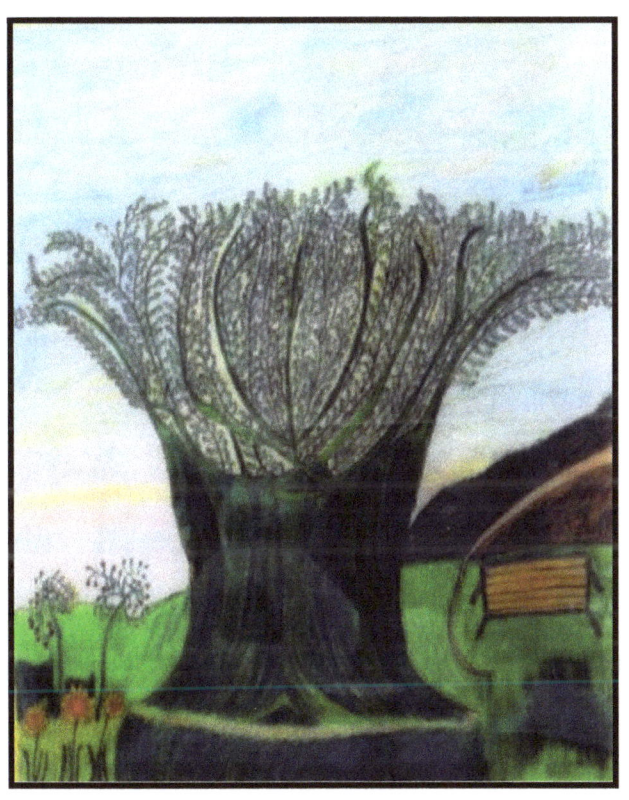

Artist
Carolyn Faye Uzzell

Art For The Soul

Photo Book ISBN: 978-1-387-63248-0

Art for the Soul

Beautiful Art that captivates the eyes of the soul!

Carolyn's *Art For The Soul* -Inspirational **Artwork that touches the soul and captivates the eye! The beauty of shared passion released! Art Expresses what we want to say but can't always put into words so the artist speaks its creation into existence by creating colorful fragrance draped on canvas!**

Carolyn's *Art For The Soul* **expresses the heart of Carolyn, the vibrant colors portrayed in her various pieces reveals her inner soul. She enjoys nature and inspirational art. She creates various pieces that reflect the eyes of the beholder and the beautiful Masterpiece God created which is the beauty of the earth.**

Contents

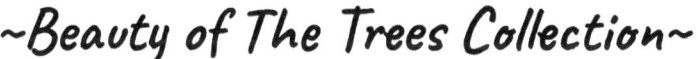

~Beauty of The Trees Collection~

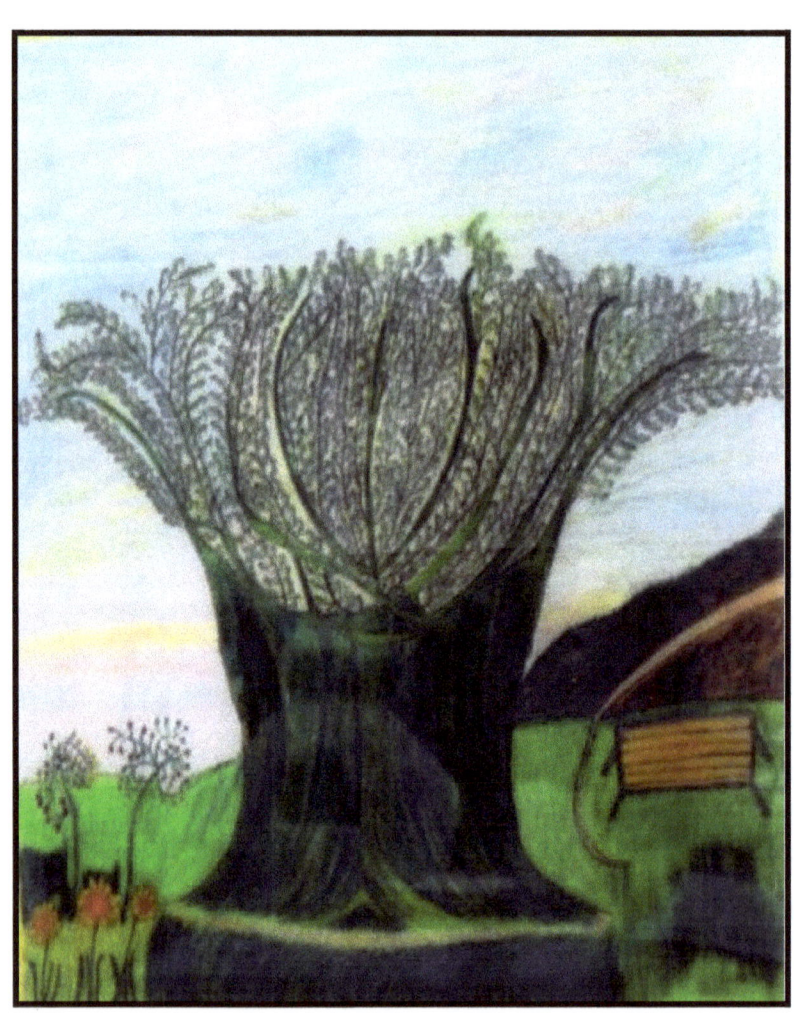

Created By Carolyn Faye Uzzell
1.

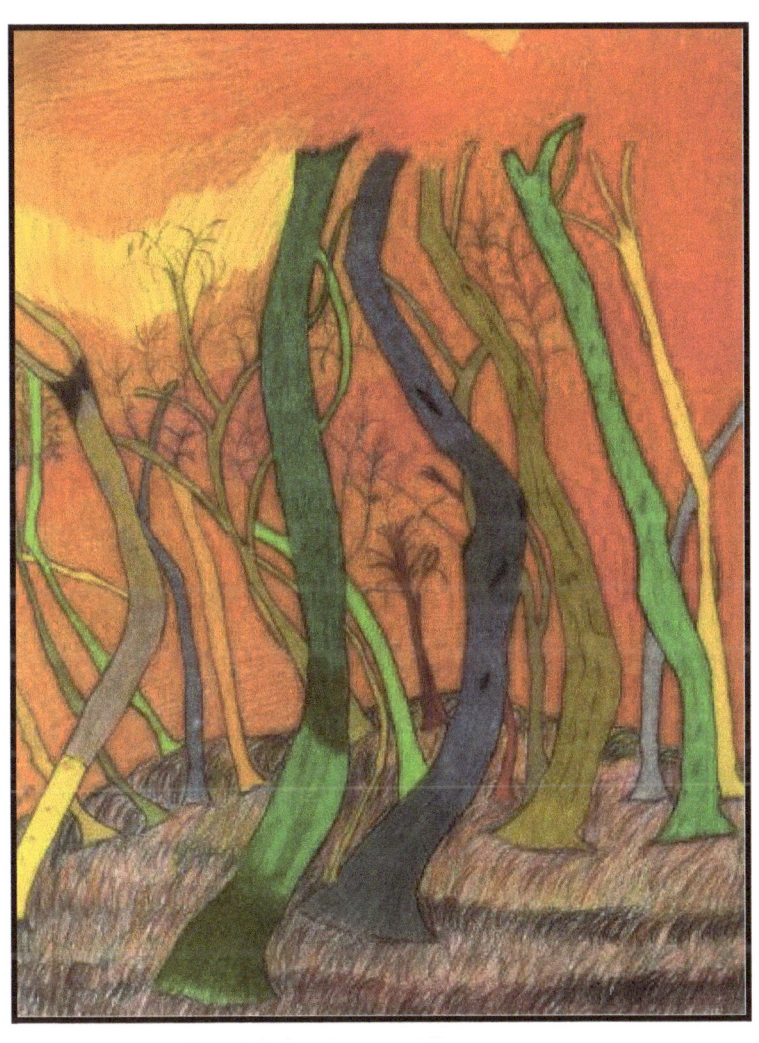

Created By Carolyn Faye Uzzell
2.

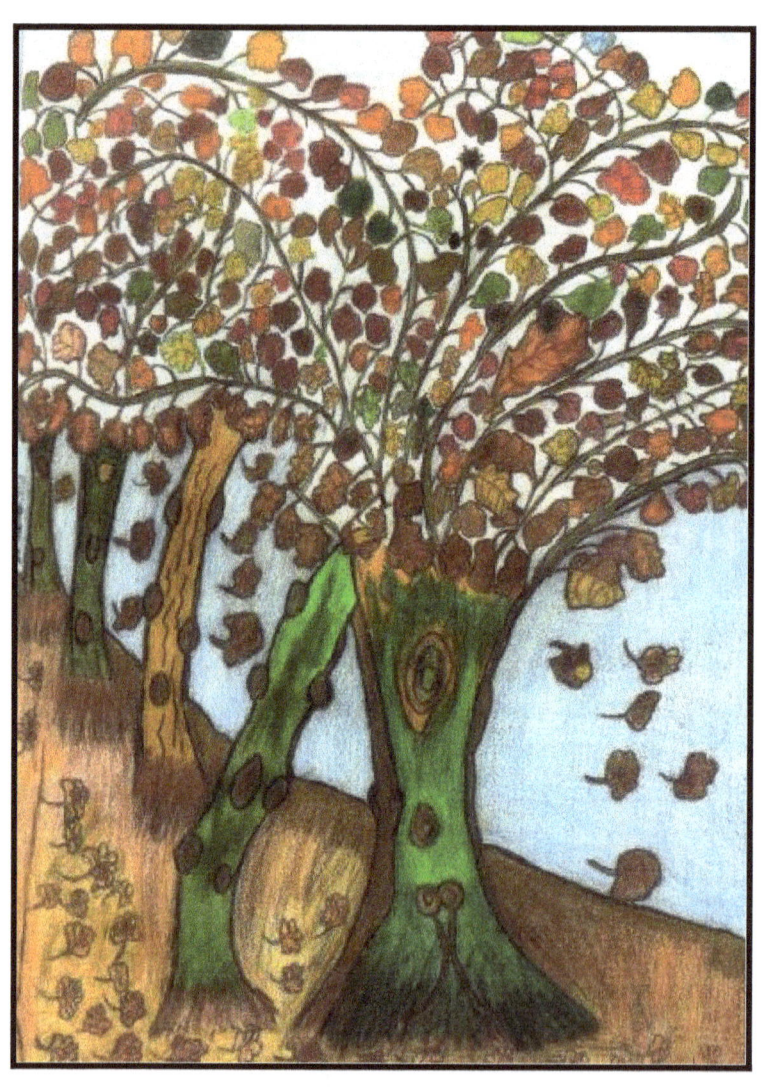

Created By Carolyn Faye Uzzell

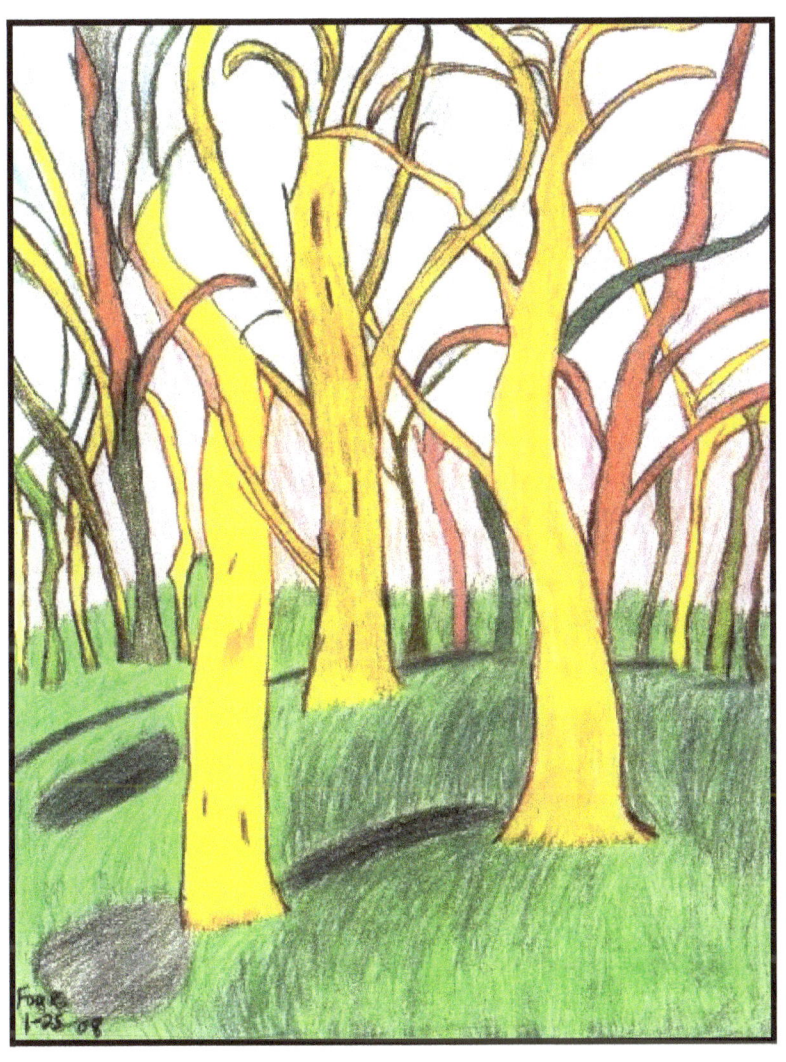

Created By Carolyn Faye Uzzell

4.

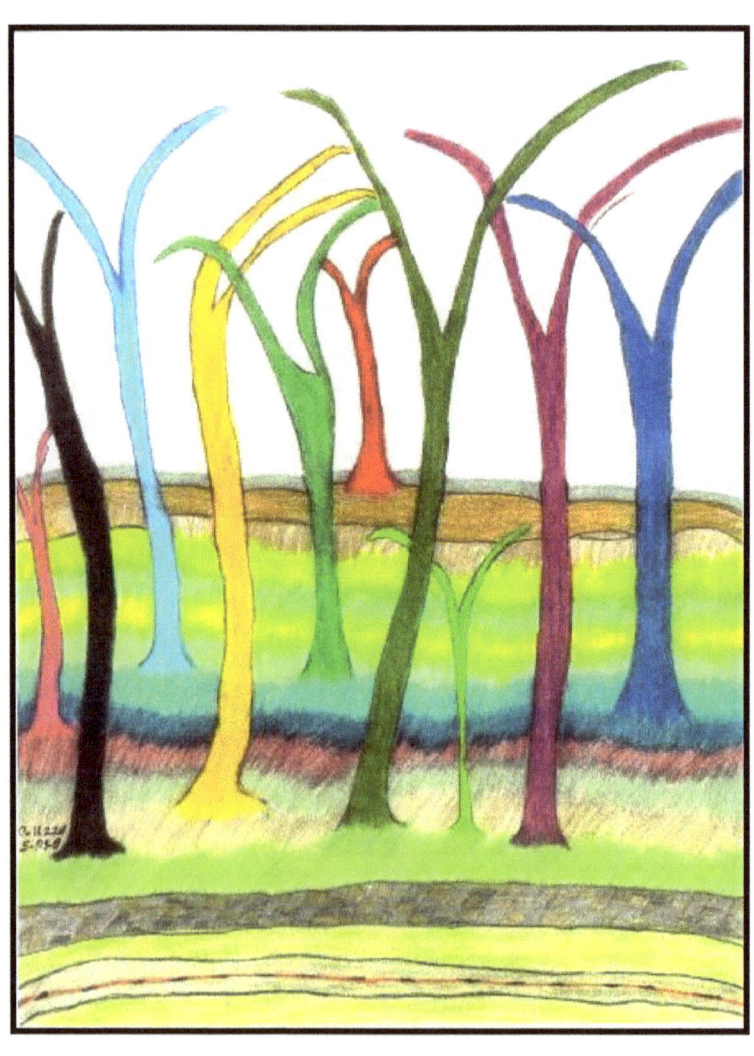

Created By Carolyn Faye Uzzell
5.

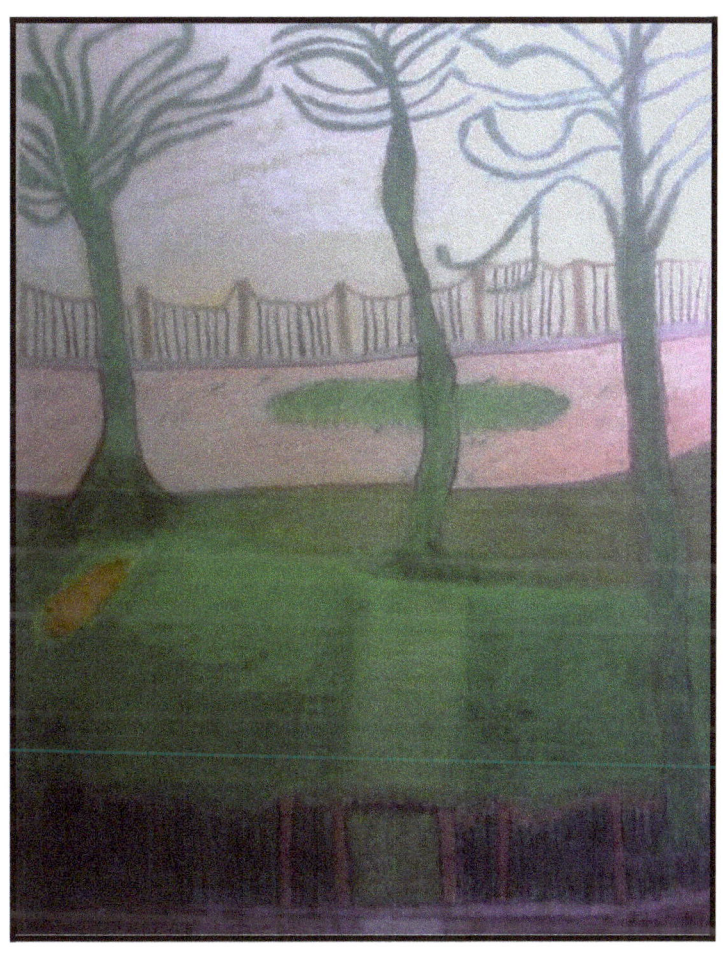

Created By Carolyn Faye Uzzell

6.

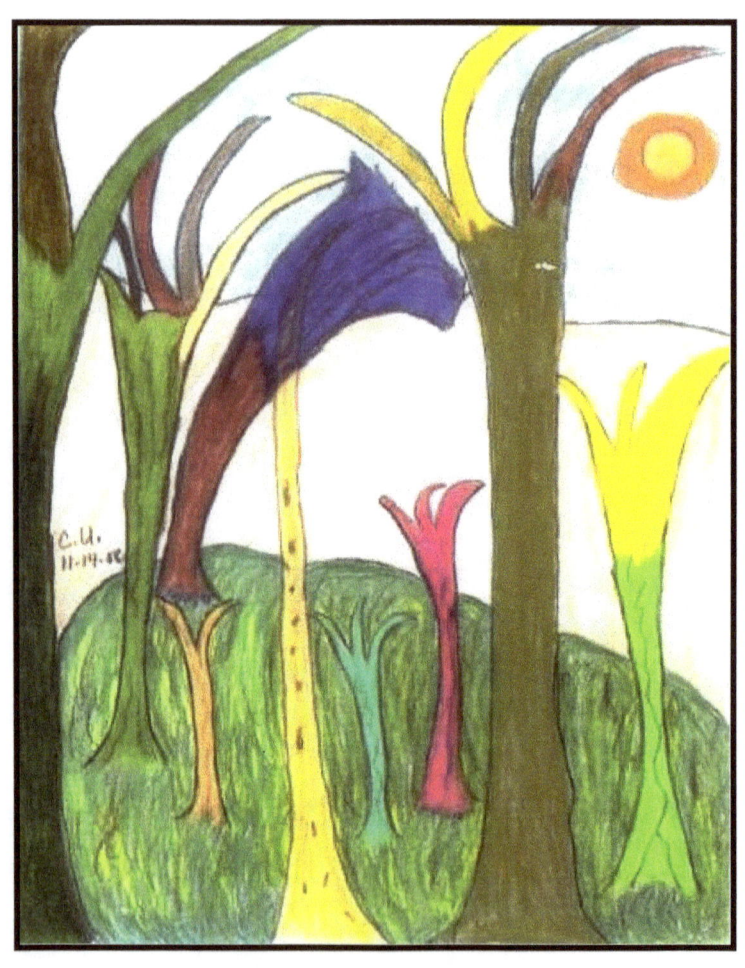

Created By Carolyn Faye Uzzell
7.

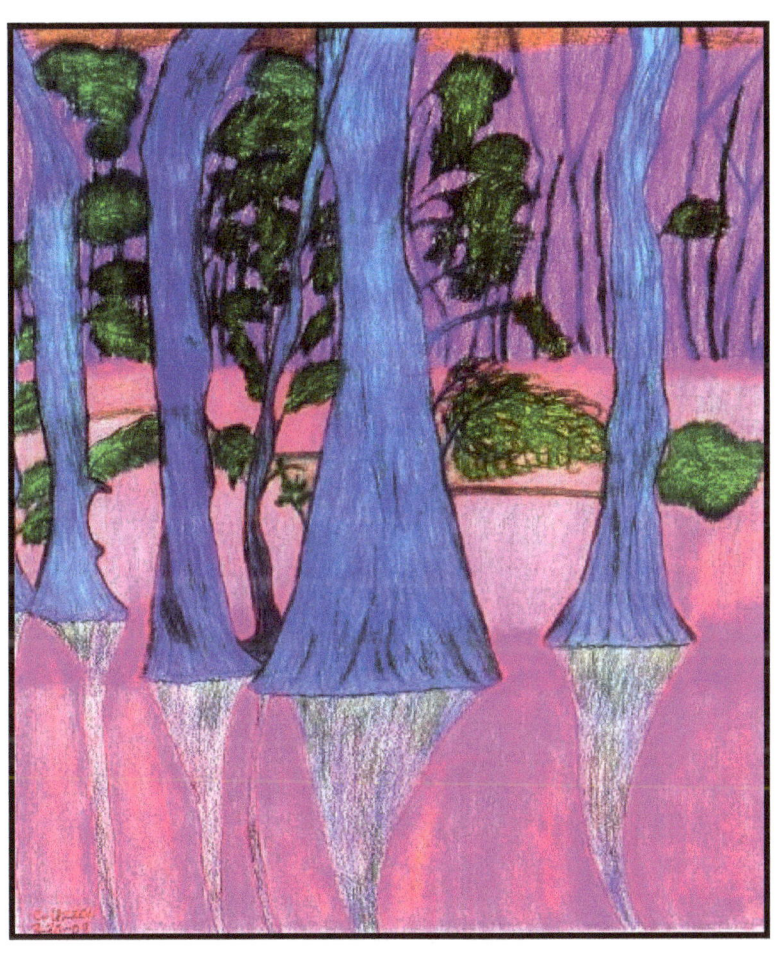

Created By Carolyn Faye Uzzell

8.

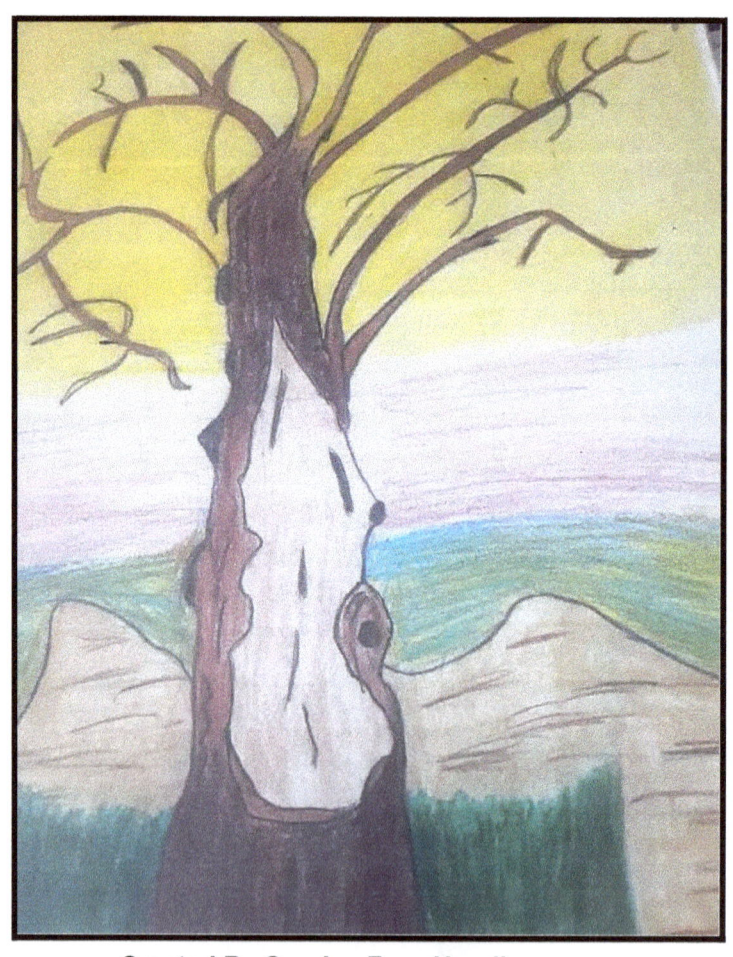

Created By Carolyn Faye Uzzell
9.

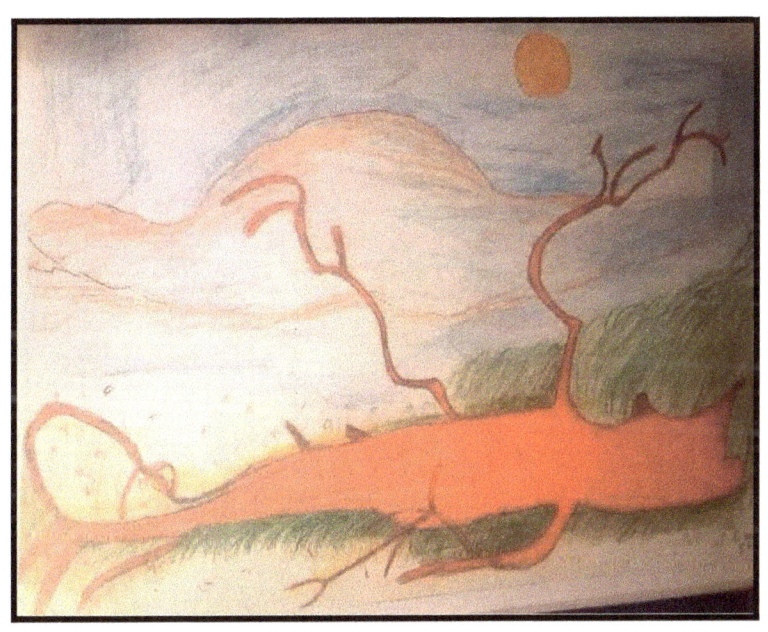

Created By Carolyn Faye Uzzell
10.

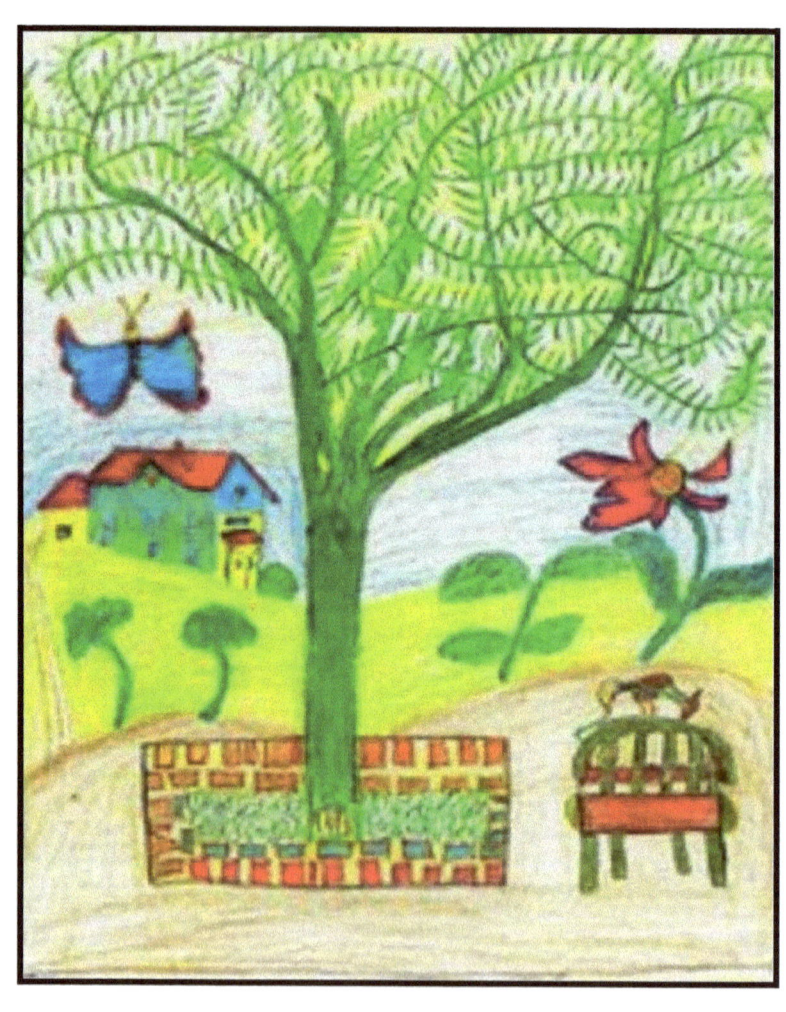

Created By Carolyn Faye Uzzell
11.

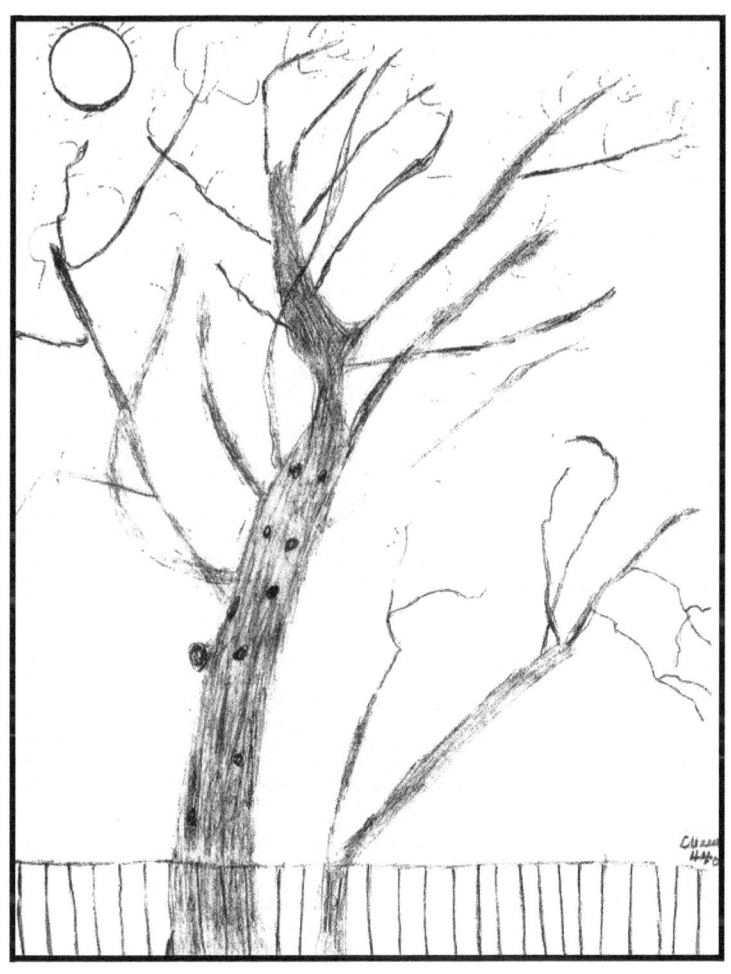

Created By Carolyn Faye Uzzell
12.

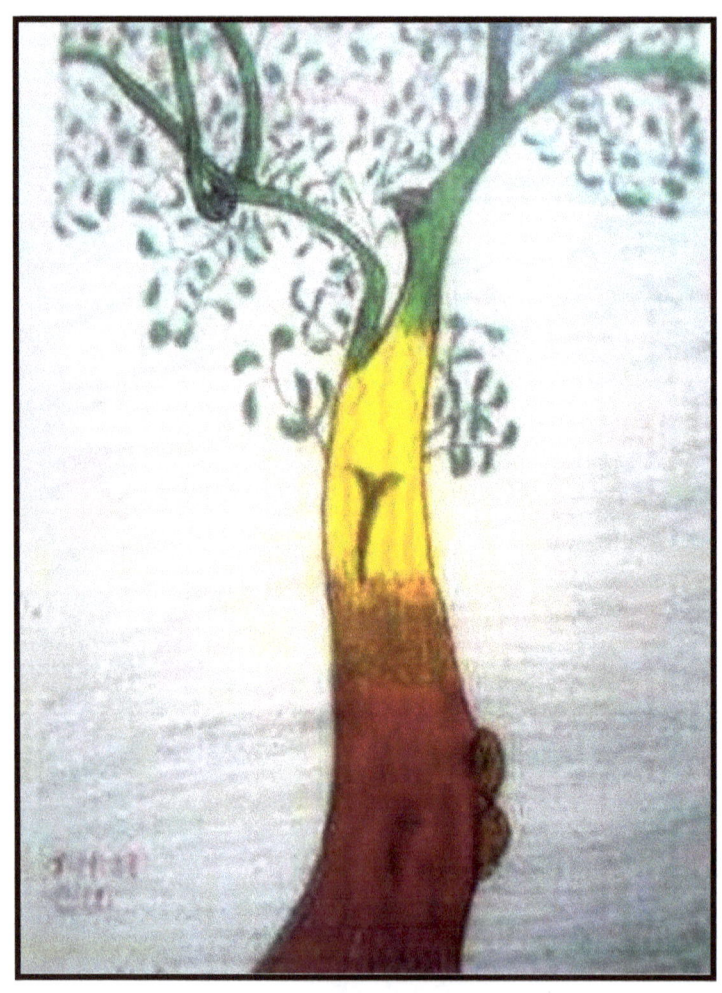

Created By Carolyn Faye Uzzell
13.

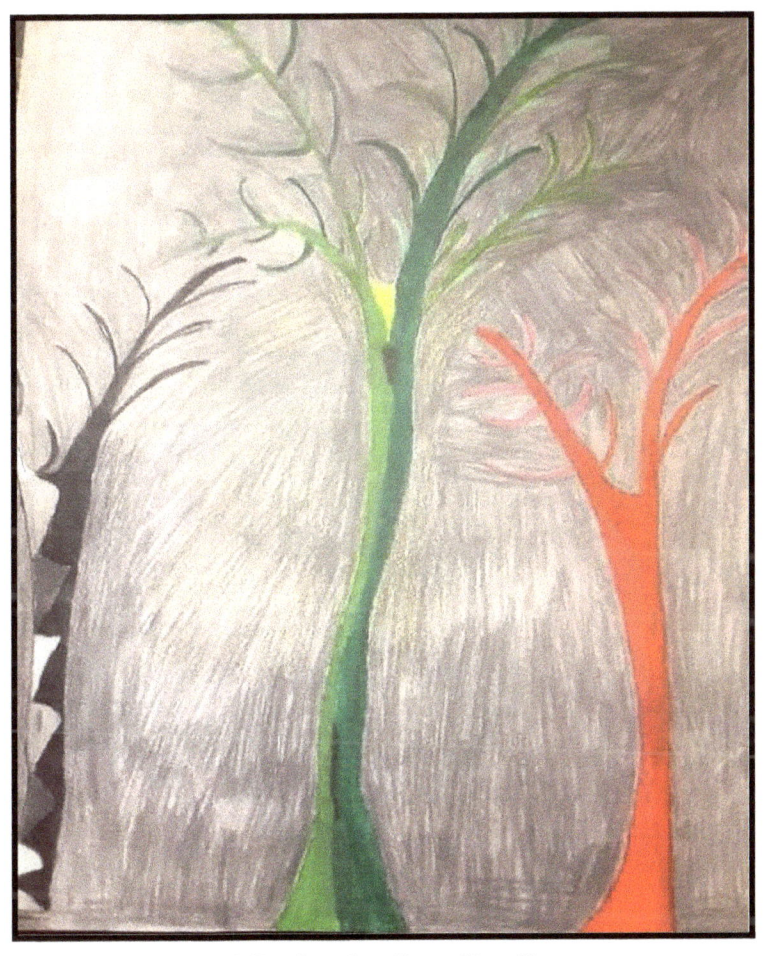

Created By Carolyn Faye Uzzell
14.

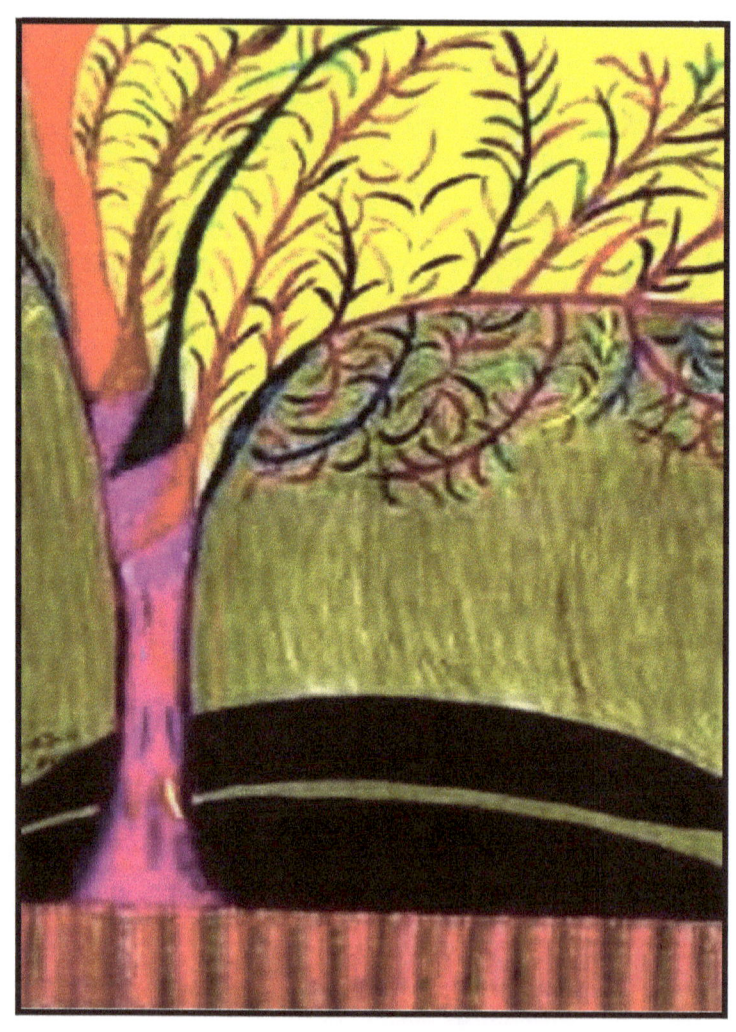

Created By Carolyn Faye Uzzell

15.

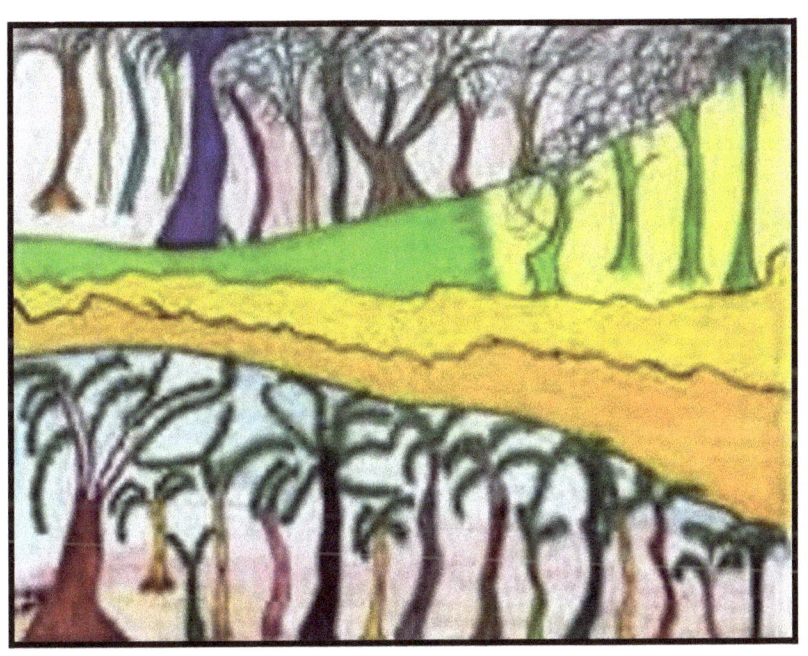

Created By Carolyn Faye Uzzell
16.

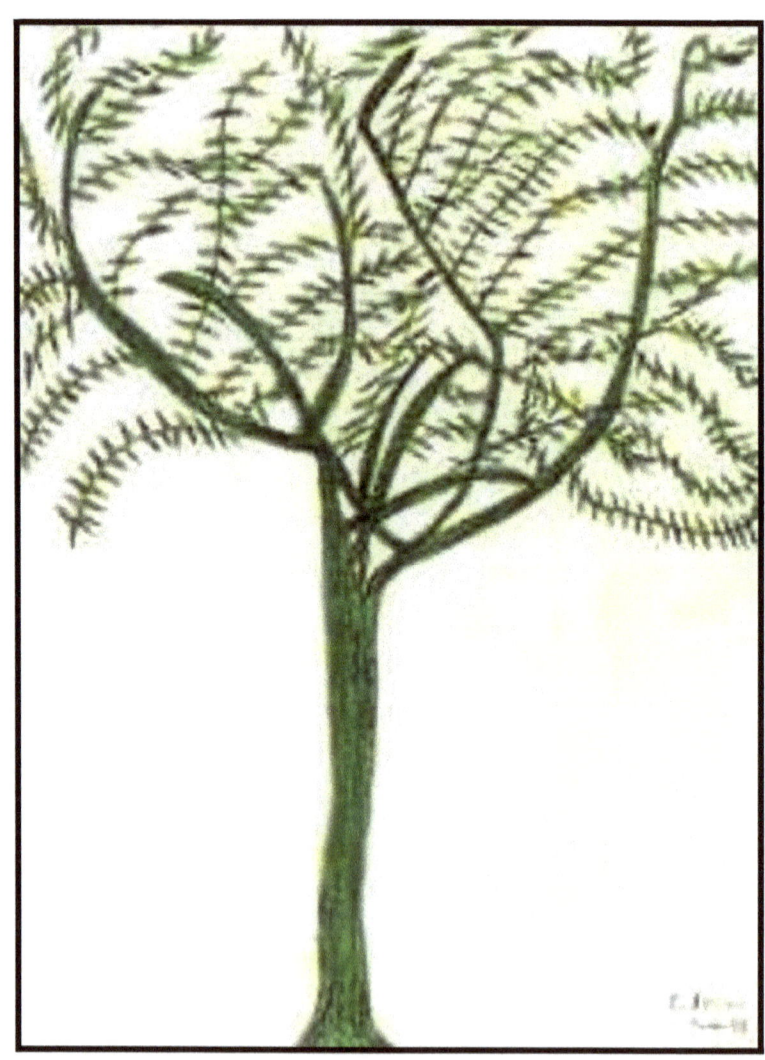

Created By Carolyn Faye Uzzell
17.

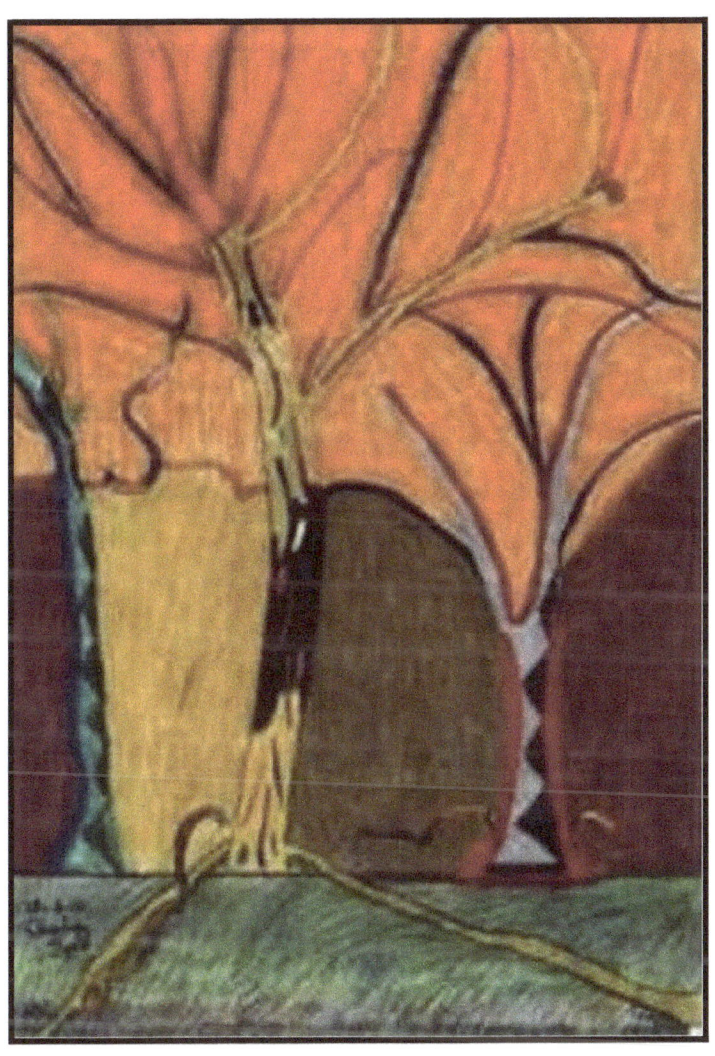

Created By Carolyn Faye Uzzell

18.

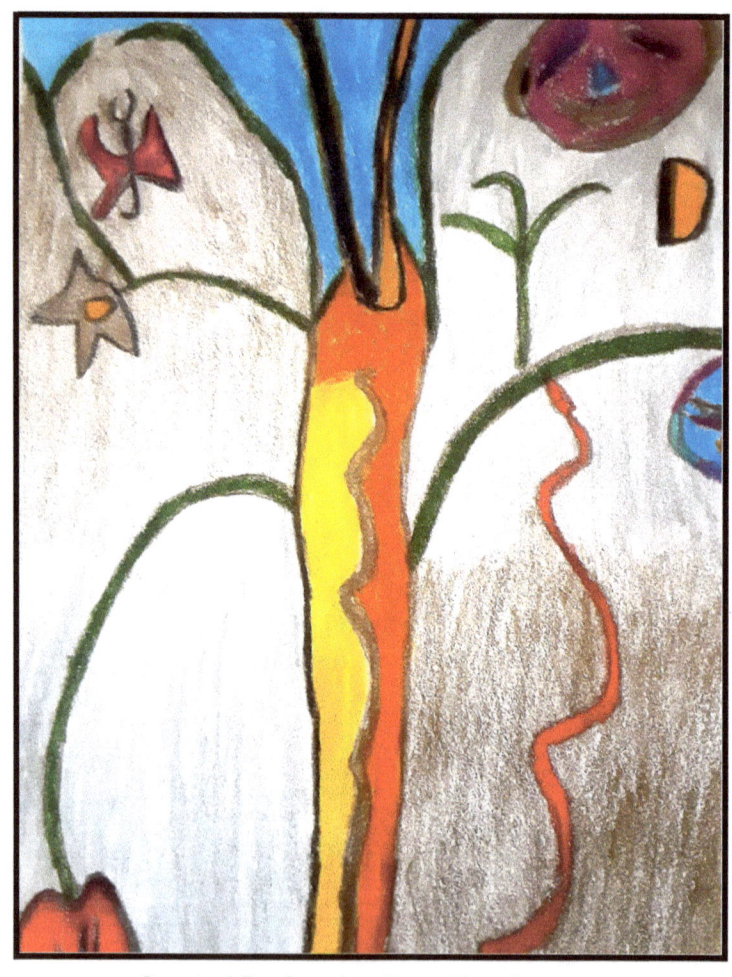

Created By Carolyn Faye Uzzel
19.

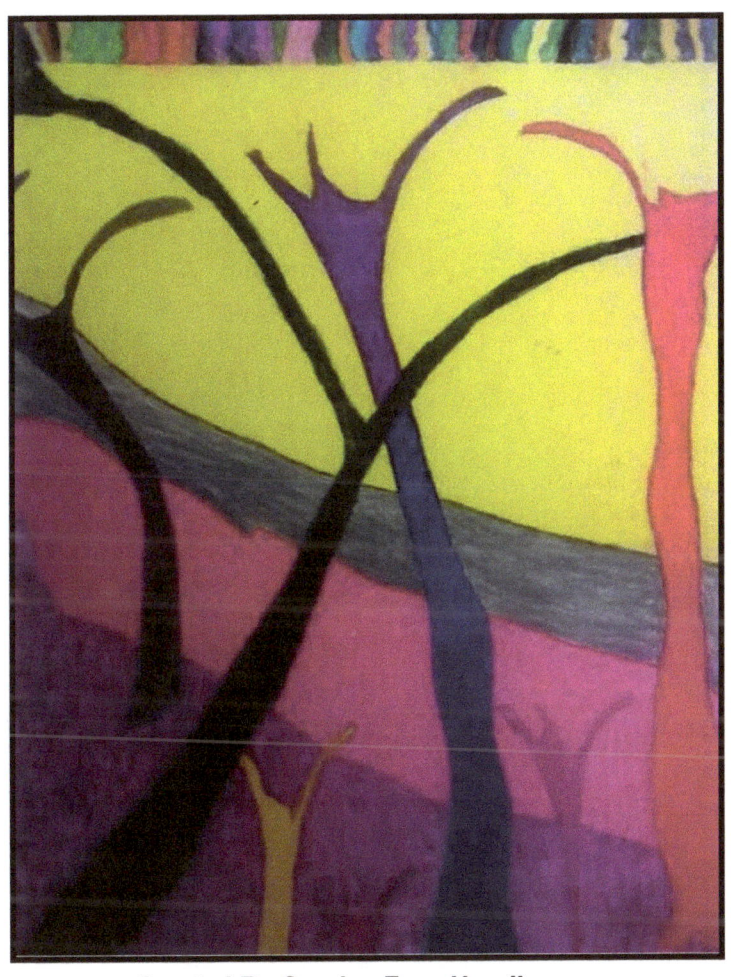

Created By Carolyn Faye Uzzell

20.

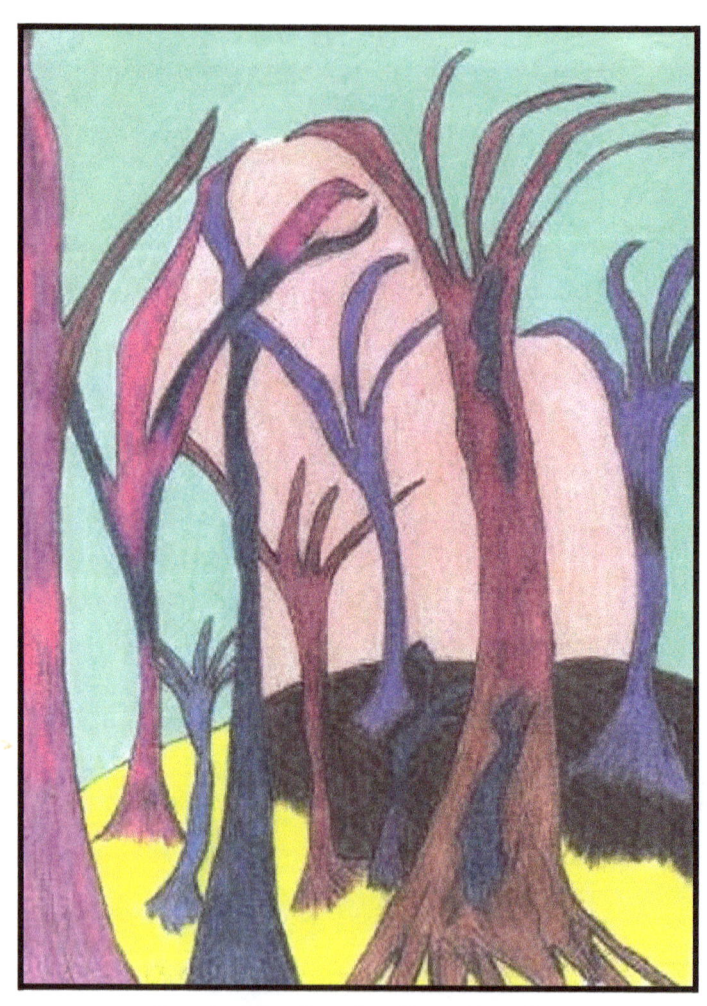

Created By Carolyn Faye Uzzell
21.

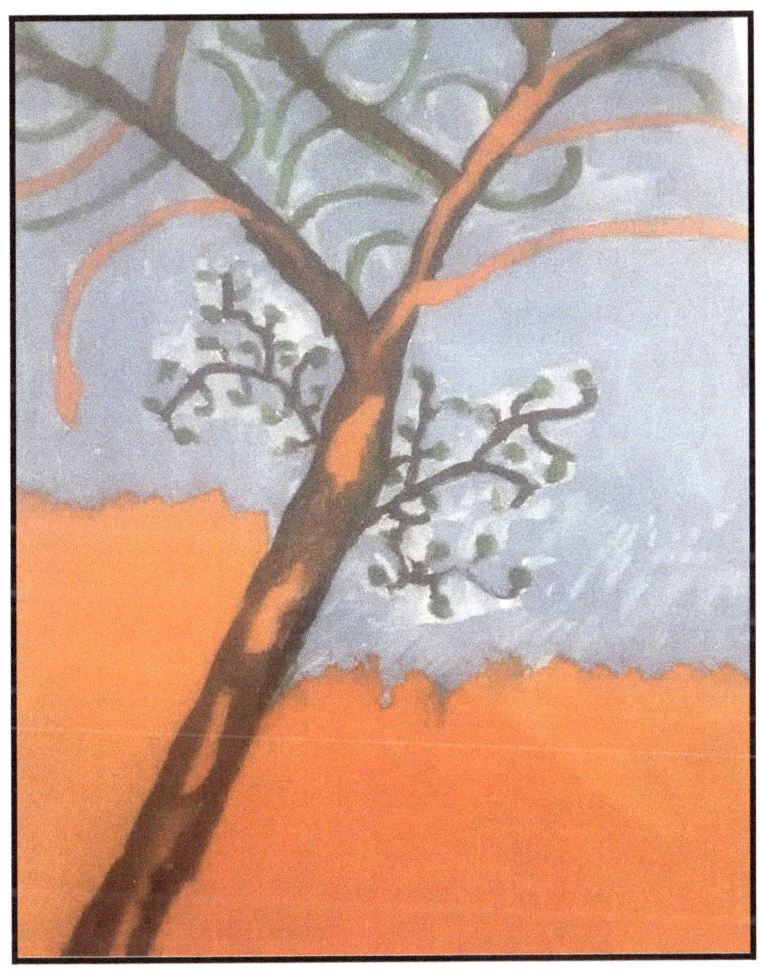

Created By Carolyn Faye Uzzell
22.

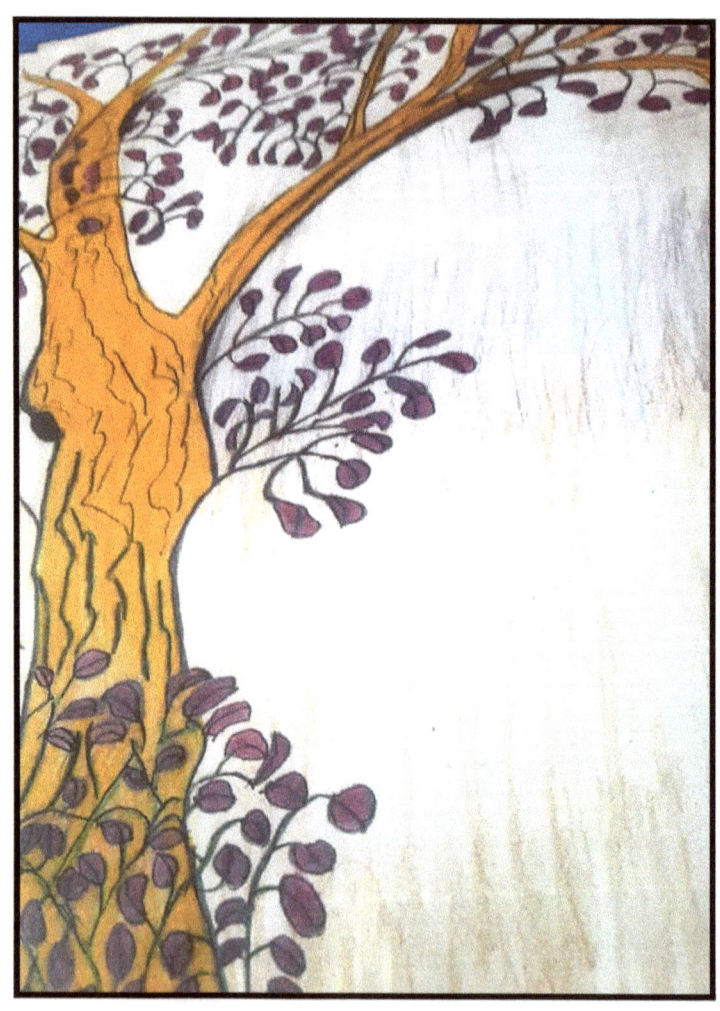

Created By Carolyn Faye Uzzell

23.

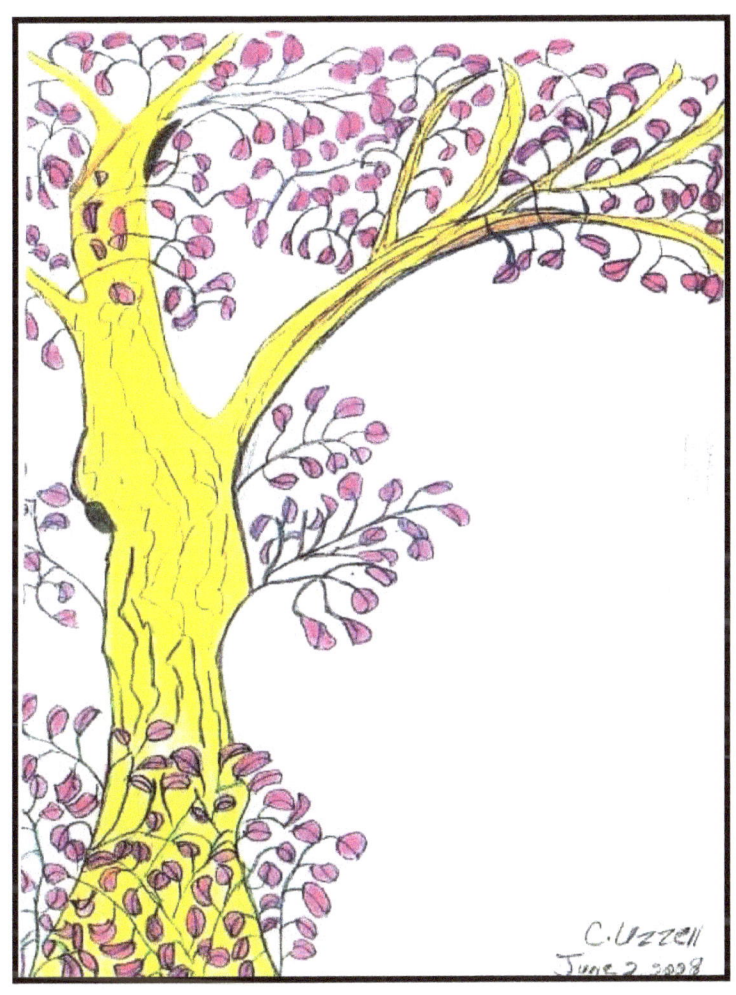

Created By Carolyn Faye Uzzell
24.

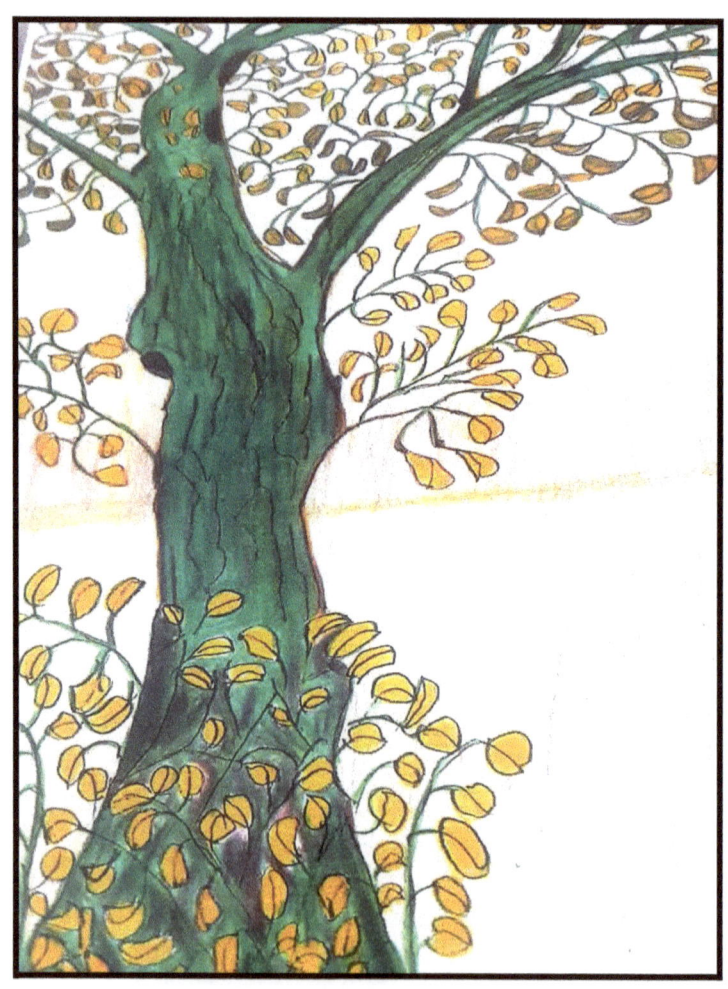

Created By Carolyn Faye Uzzell
25

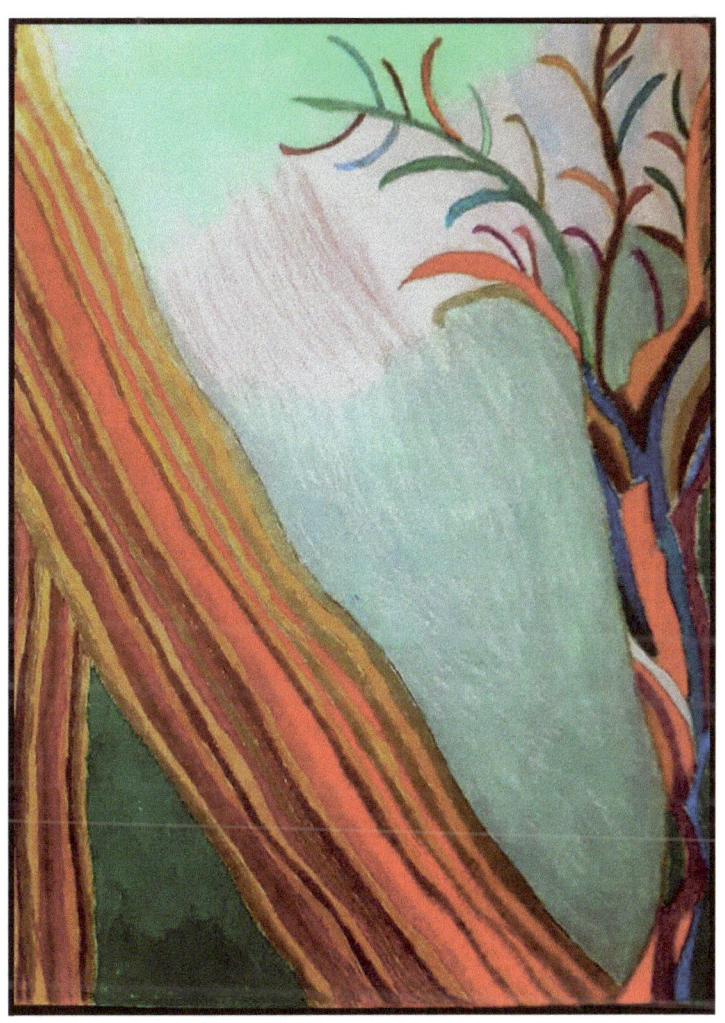

Created By Carolyn Faye Uzzell
26.

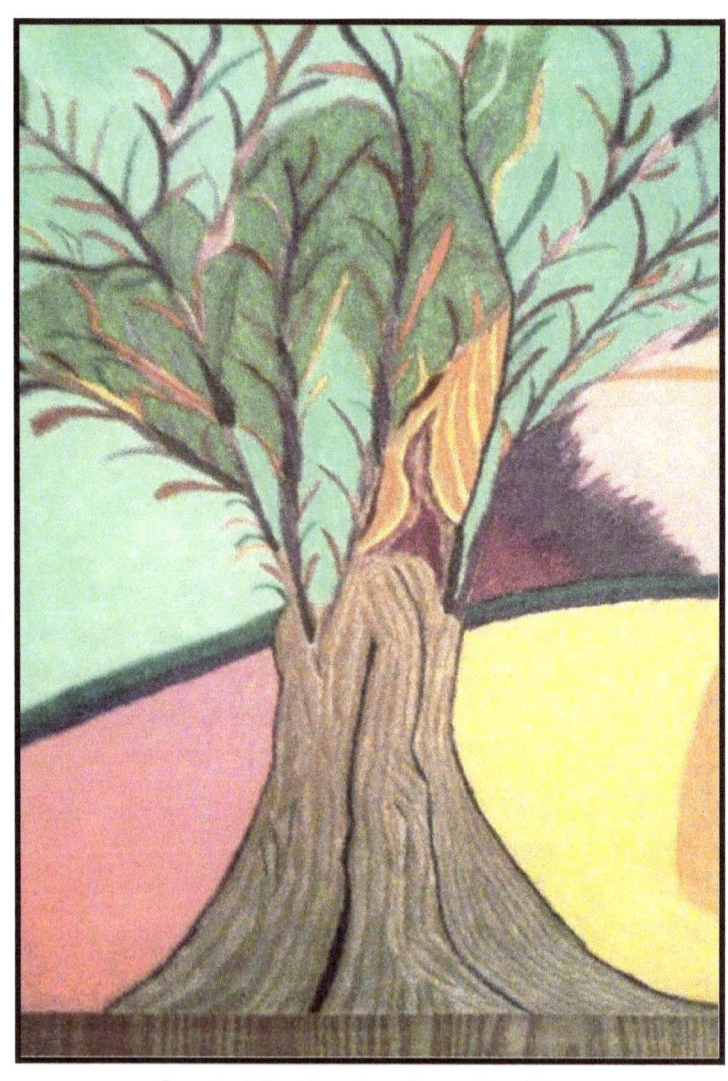

Created By Carolyn Faye Uzzell
27.

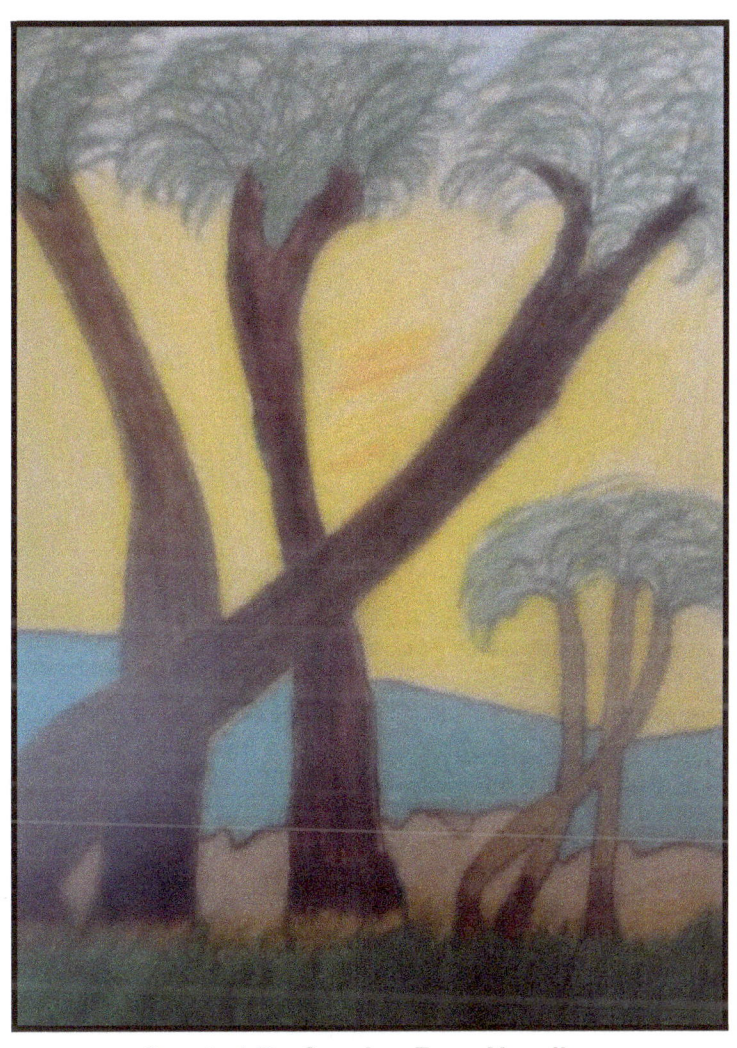

Created By Carolyn Faye Uzzell
28.

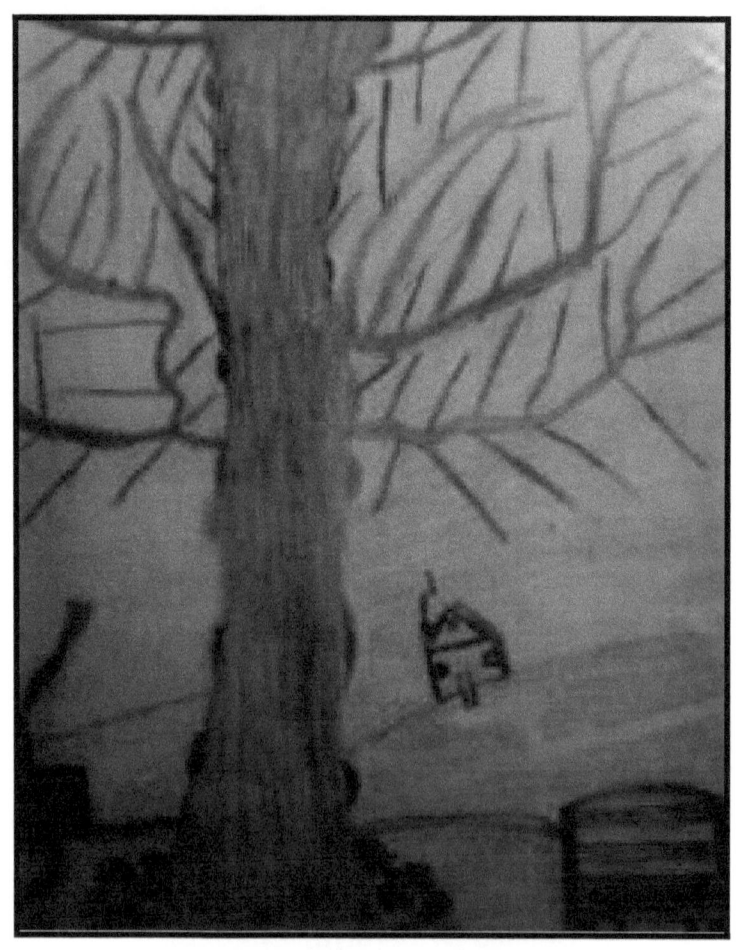

Created By Carolyn Faye Uzzell
29.

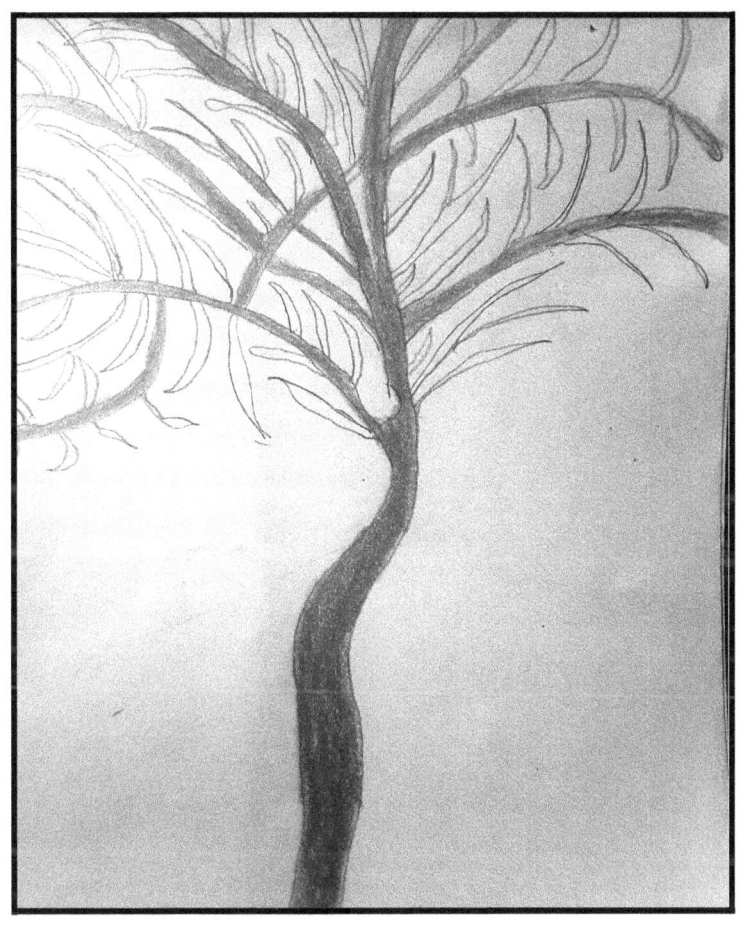

Created By Carolyn Faye Uzzell
30.

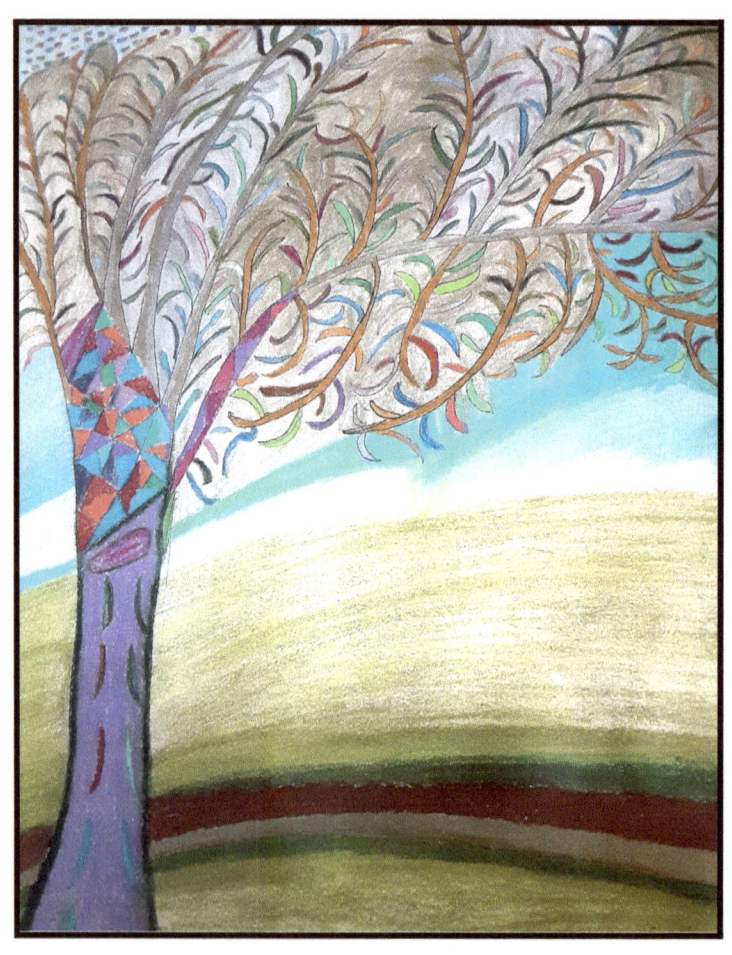

Created By Carolyn Faye Uzzell
31.

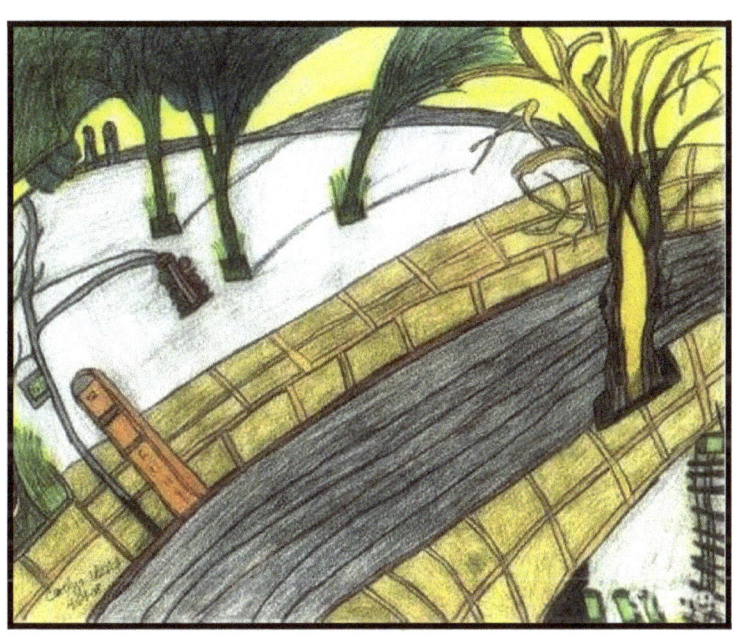

Created By Carolyn Faye Uzzell
32.

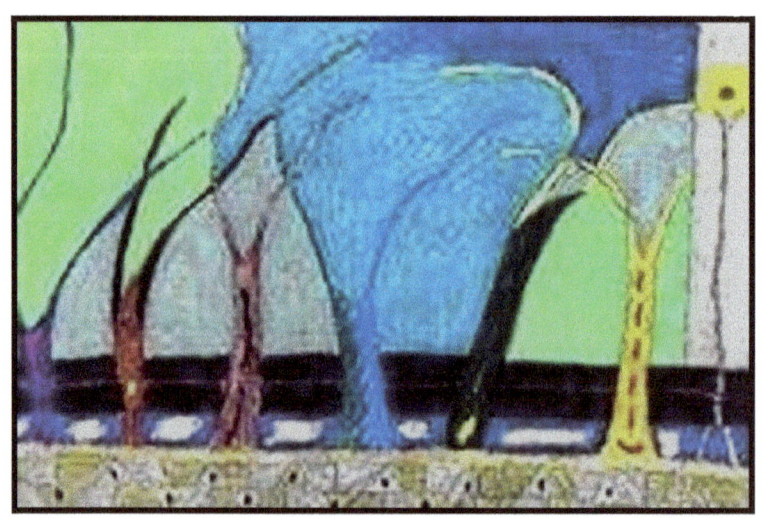

Created By Carolyn Faye Uzzell
33.

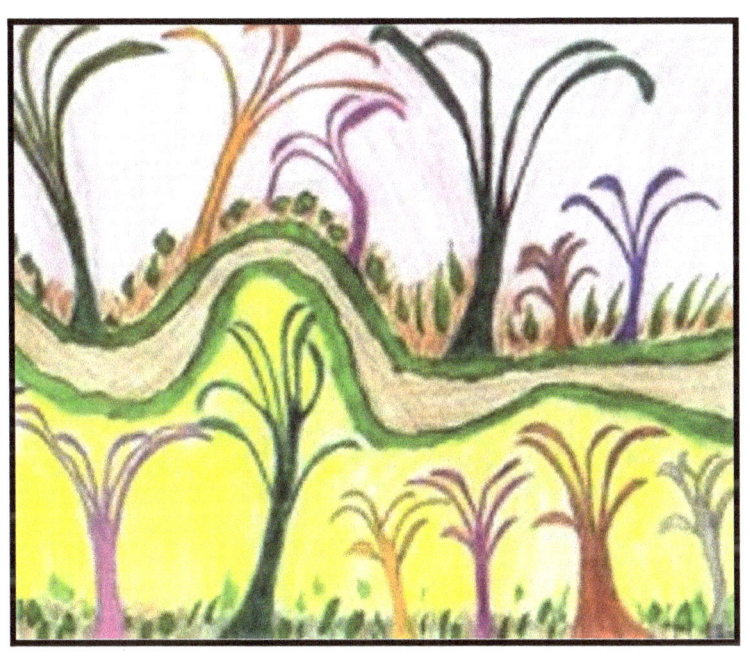

Created By Carolyn Faye Uzzell
34.

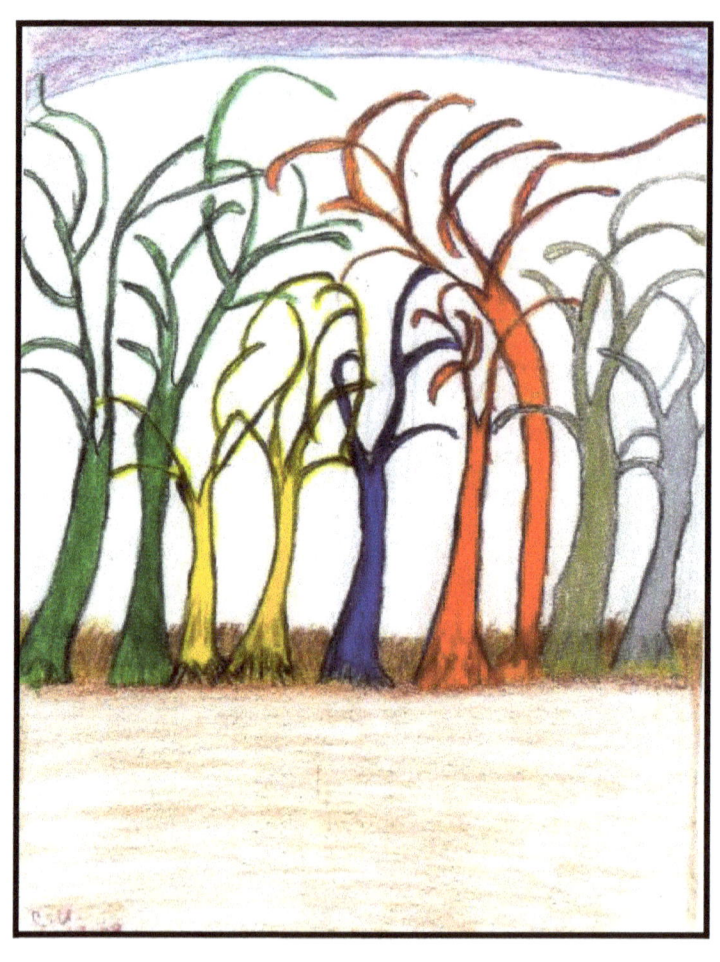

Created By Carolyn Faye Uzzell
35.

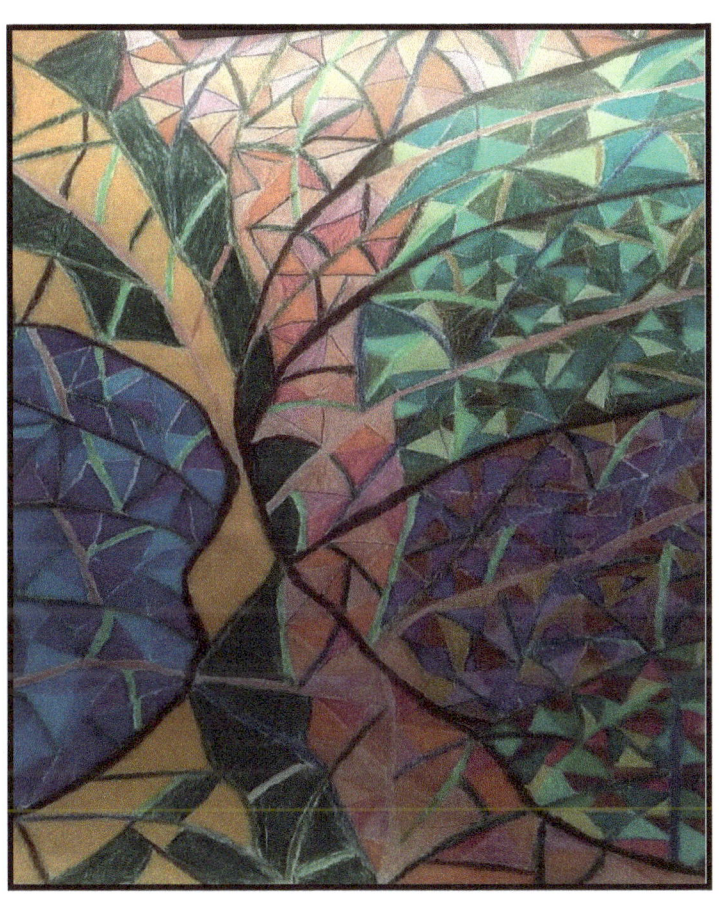

Created By Carolyn Faye Uzzell
36.

~Inspirational Art Collection ~

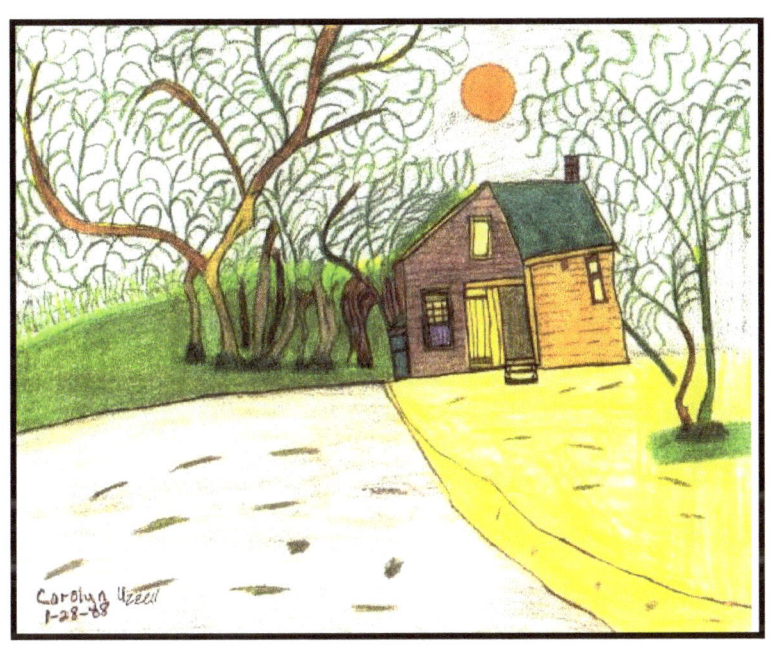

Created By Carolyn Faye Uzzell
37.

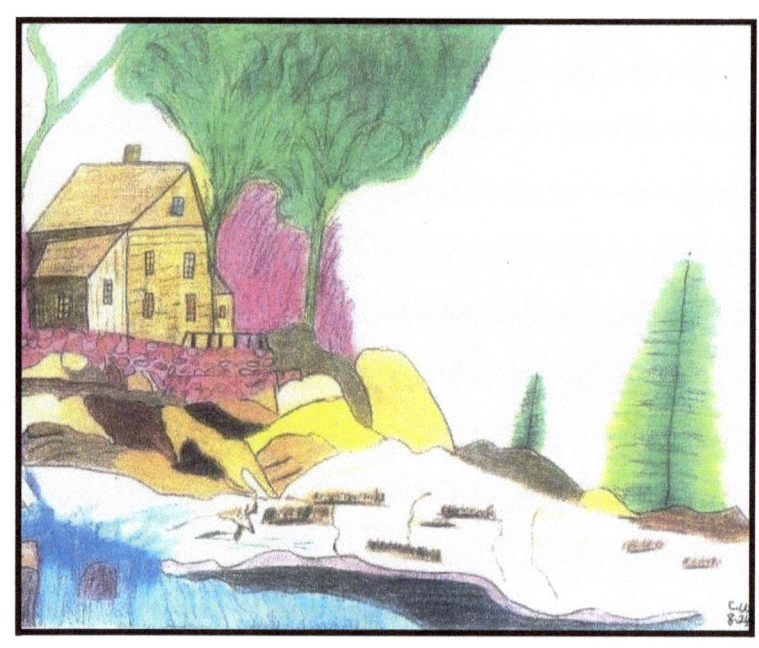

Created By Carolyn Faye Uzzell
38.

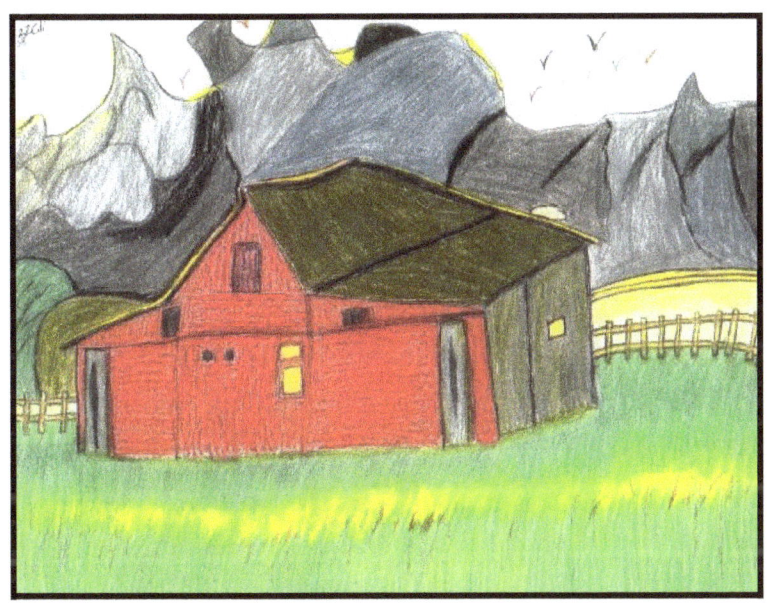

Created By Carolyn Faye Uzzell
39.

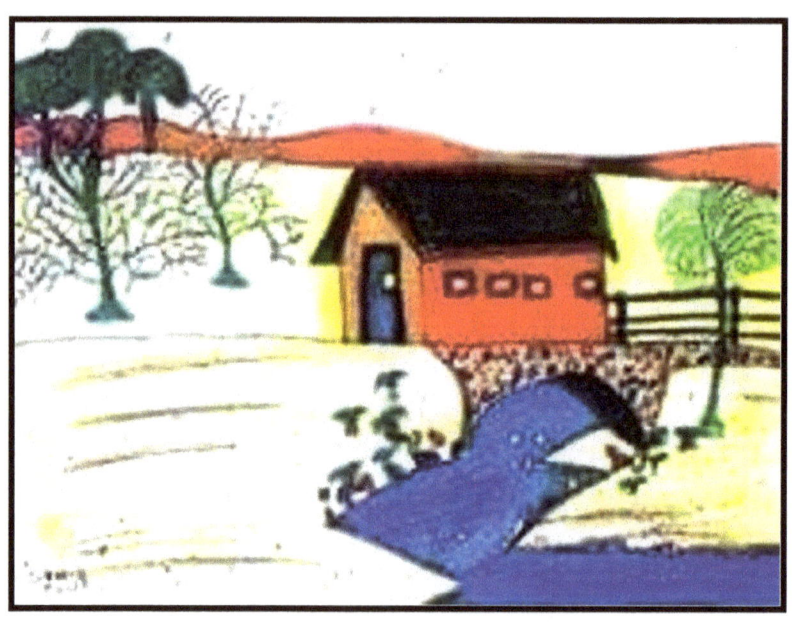

Created By Carolyn Faye Uzzell
40.

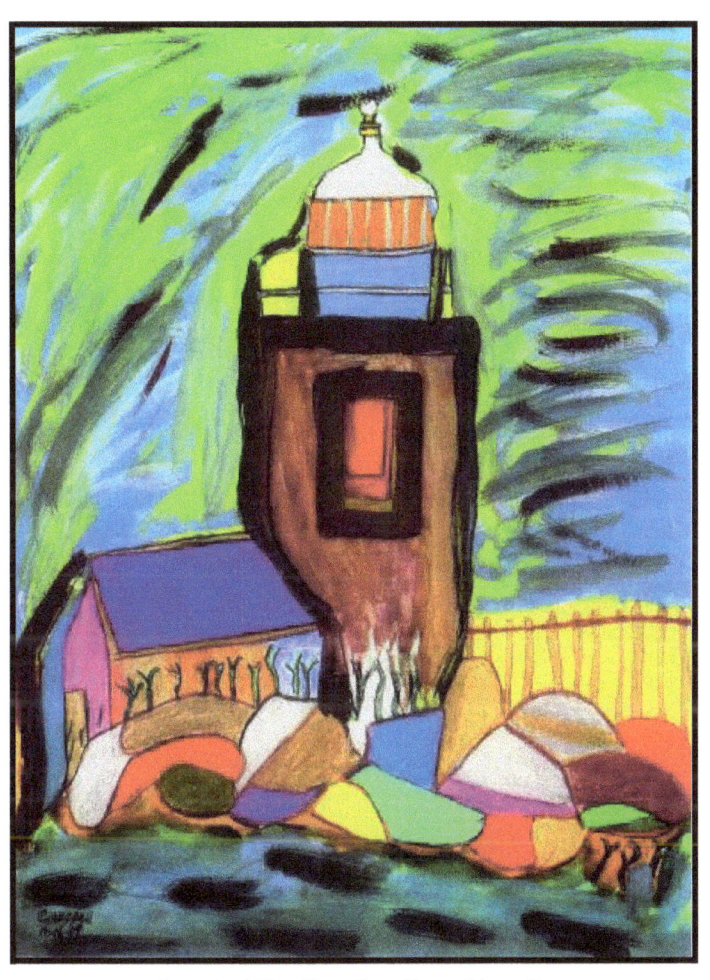

Created By Carolyn Faye Uzzell
41.

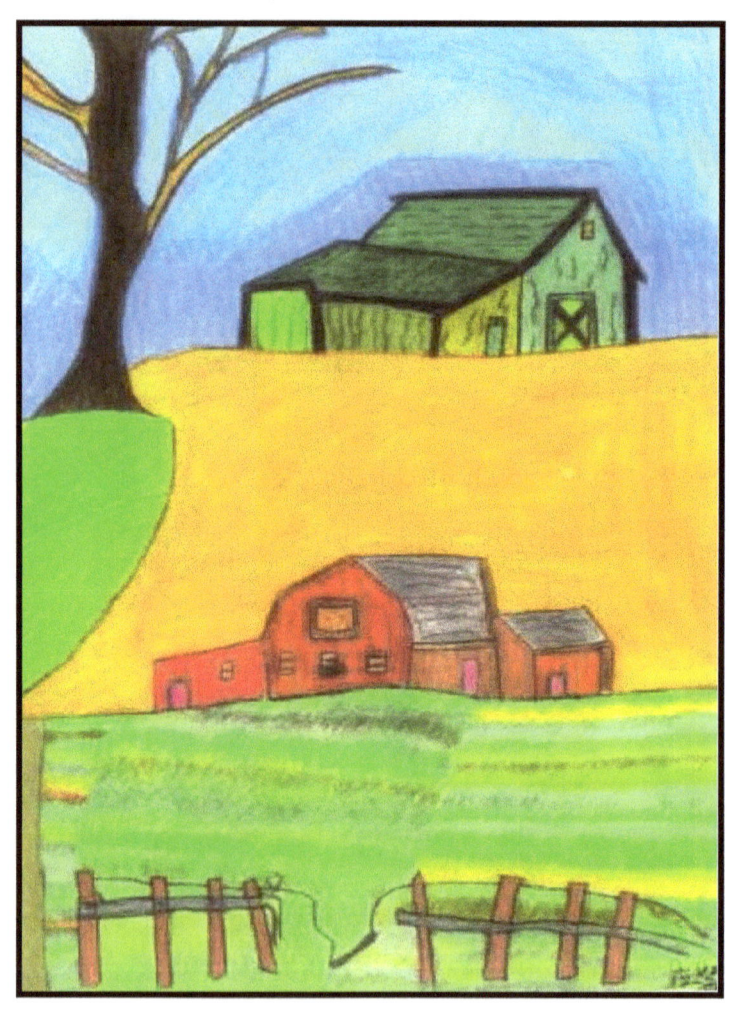

Created By Carolyn Faye Uzzell
42.

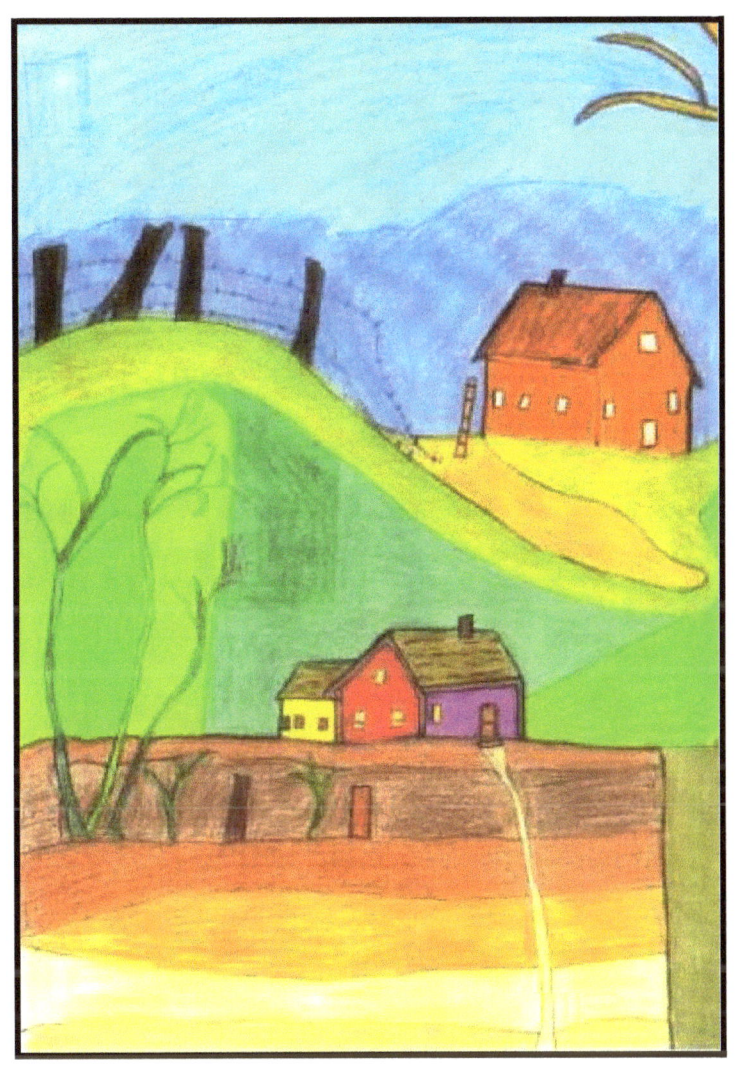

Created By Carolyn Faye Uzzell
43.

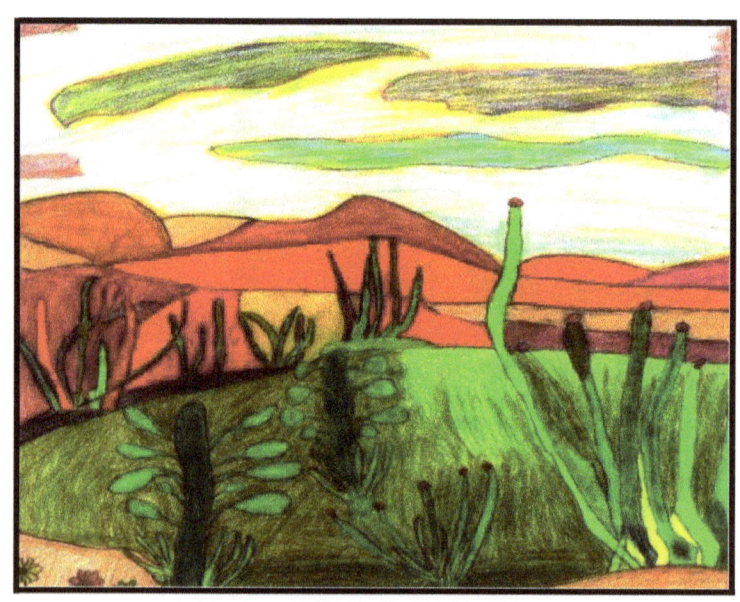

Created By Carolyn Faye Uzzell
44.

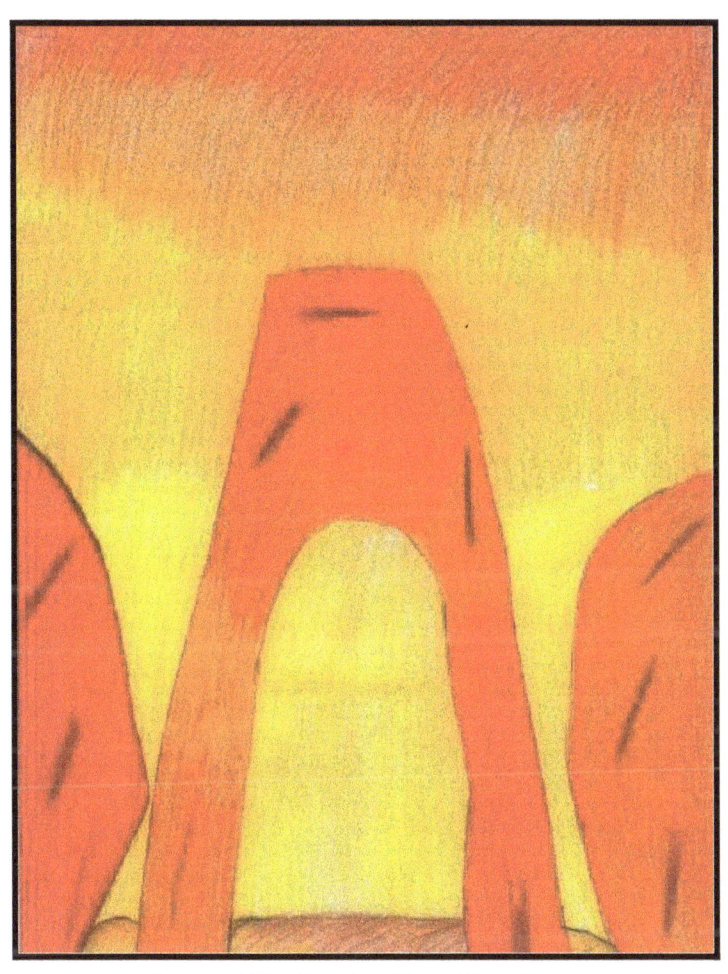

Created By Carolyn Faye Uzzell
45.

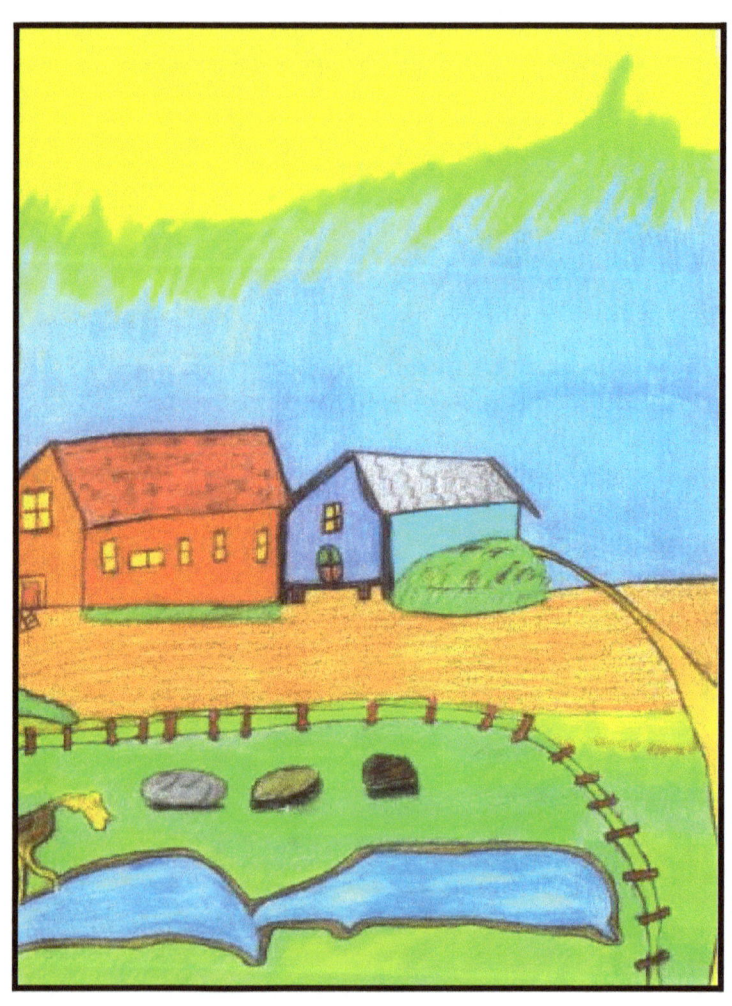

Created By Carolyn Faye Uzzell
46.

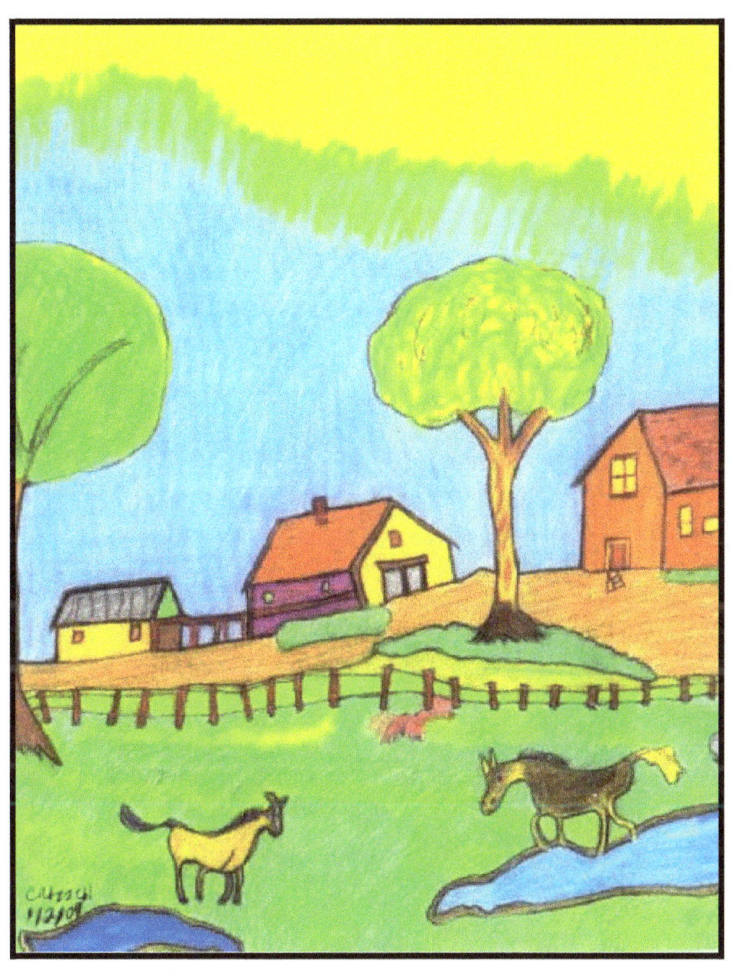

Created By Carolyn Faye Uzzell
47.

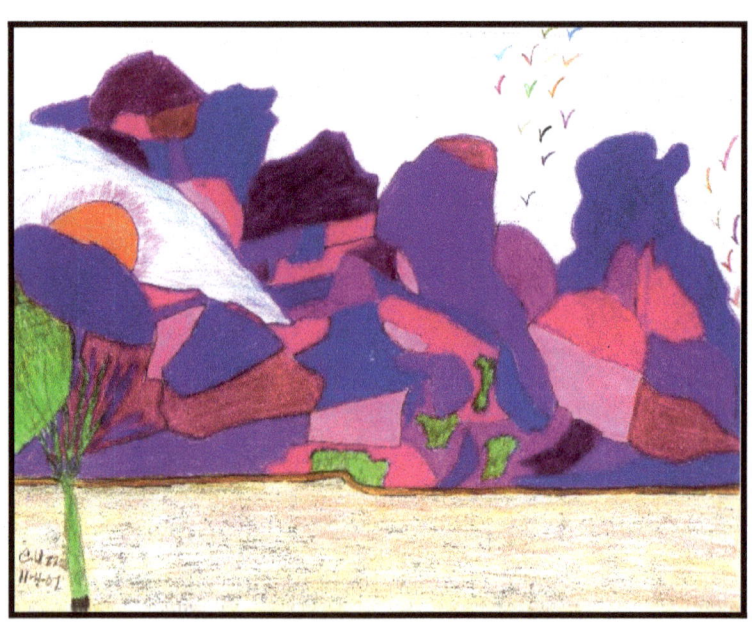

Created By Carolyn Faye Uzzell
48.

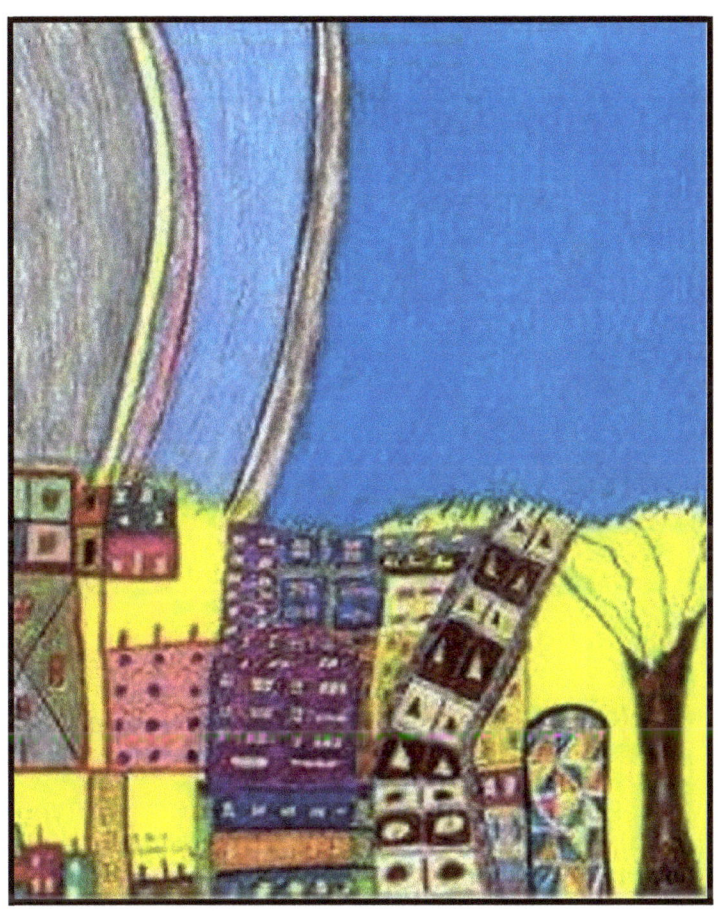

Created By Carolyn Faye Uzzell
49.

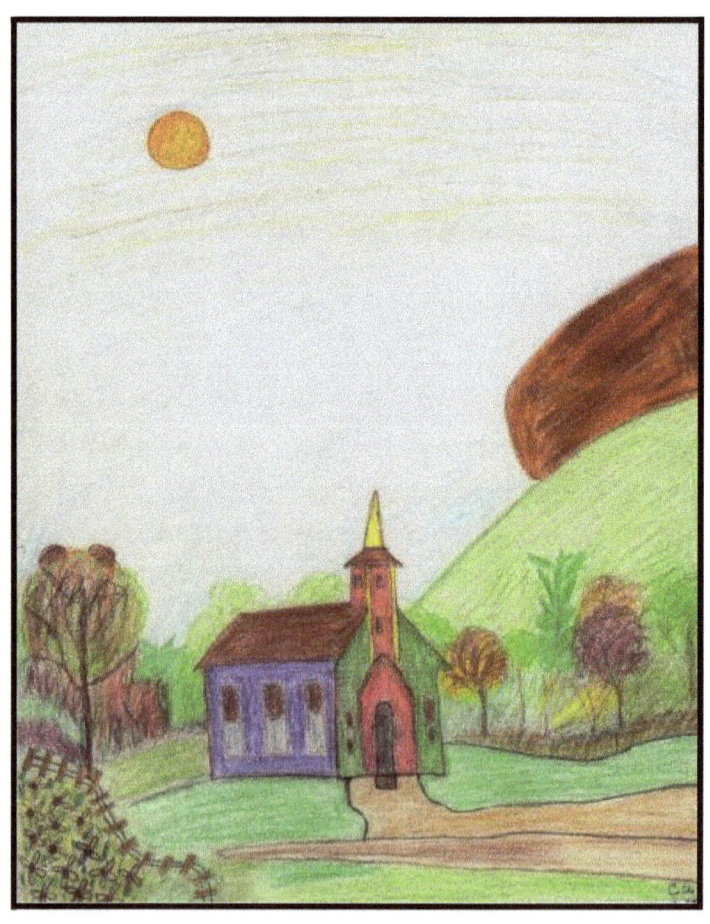

Created By Carolyn Faye Uzzel

50.

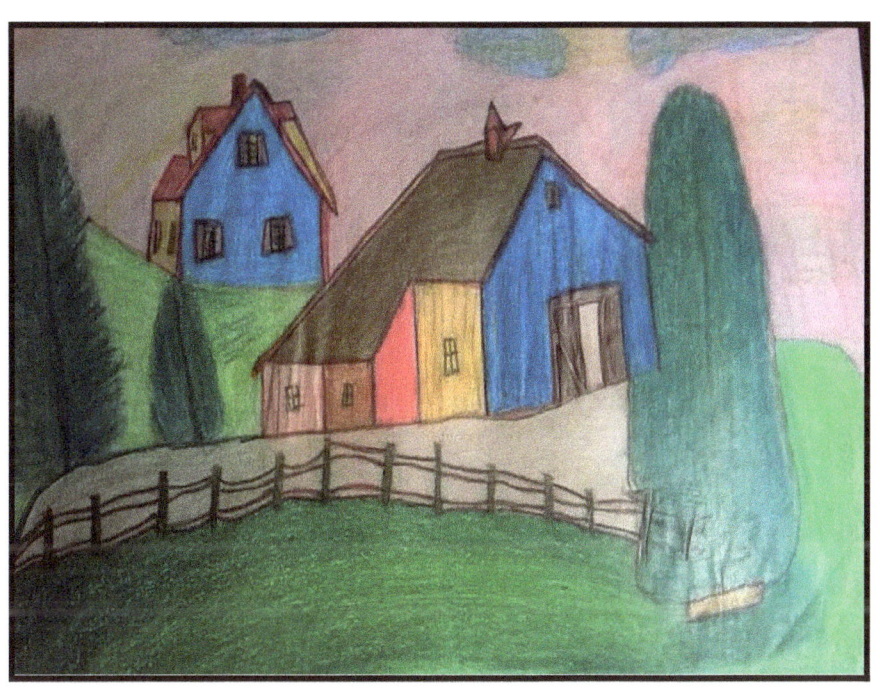

Created By Carolyn Faye Uzzell
51.

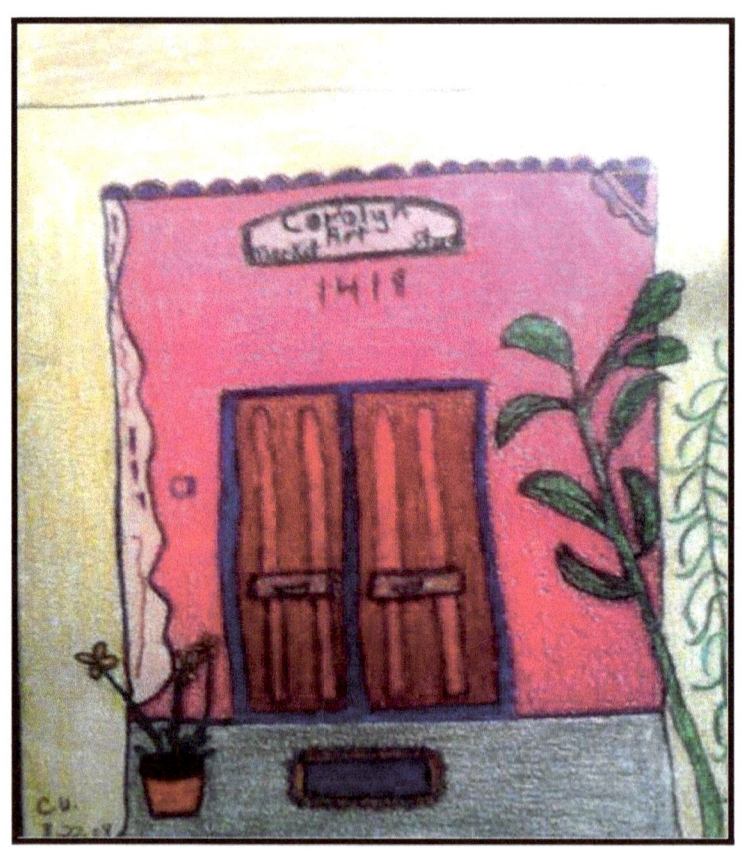

Created By Carolyn Faye Uzzell
52.

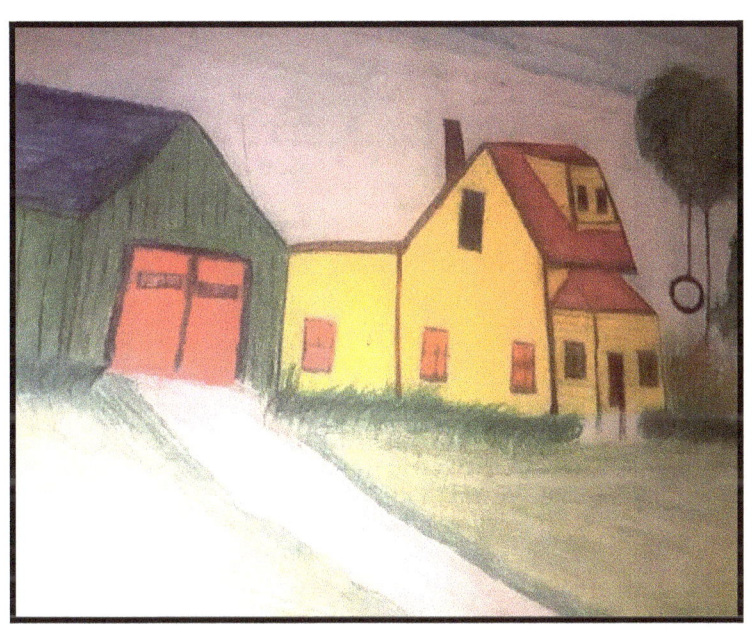

Created By Carolyn Faye Uzzell
53.

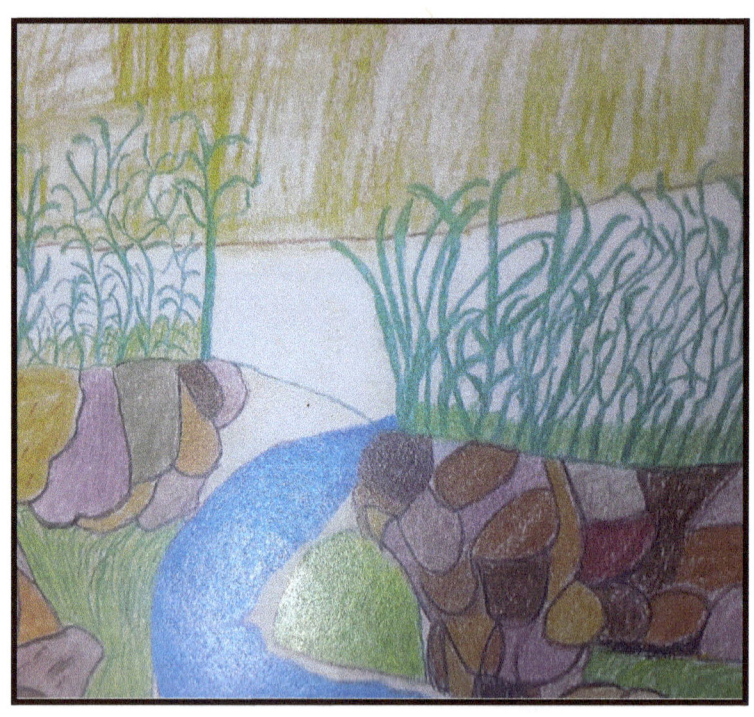

Created By Carolyn Faye Uzzell
54.

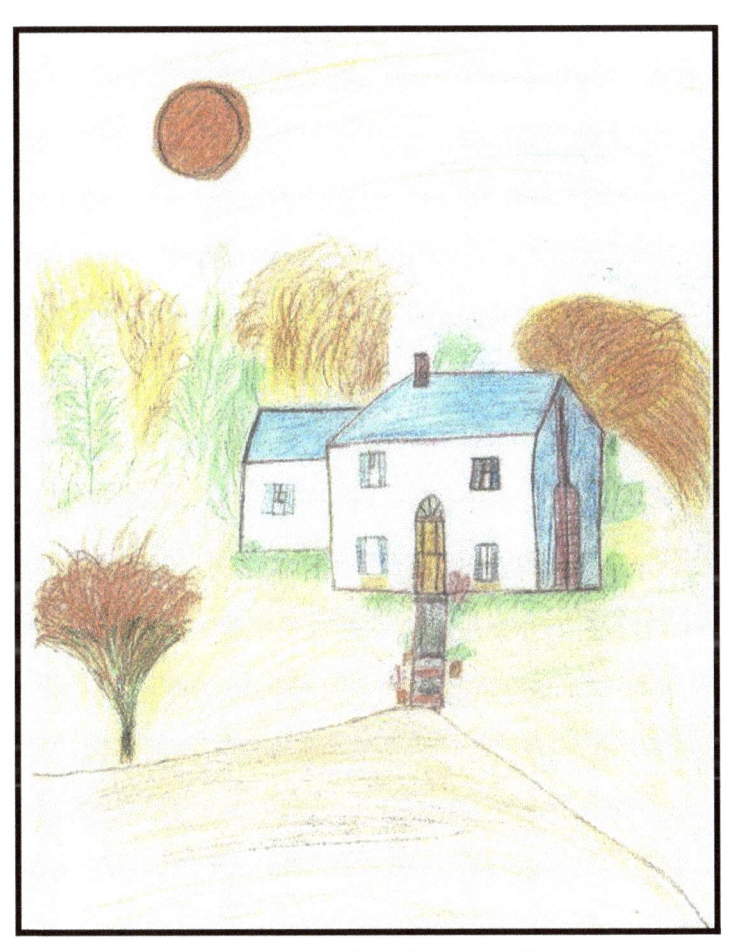

Created By Carolyn Faye Uzzell
55.

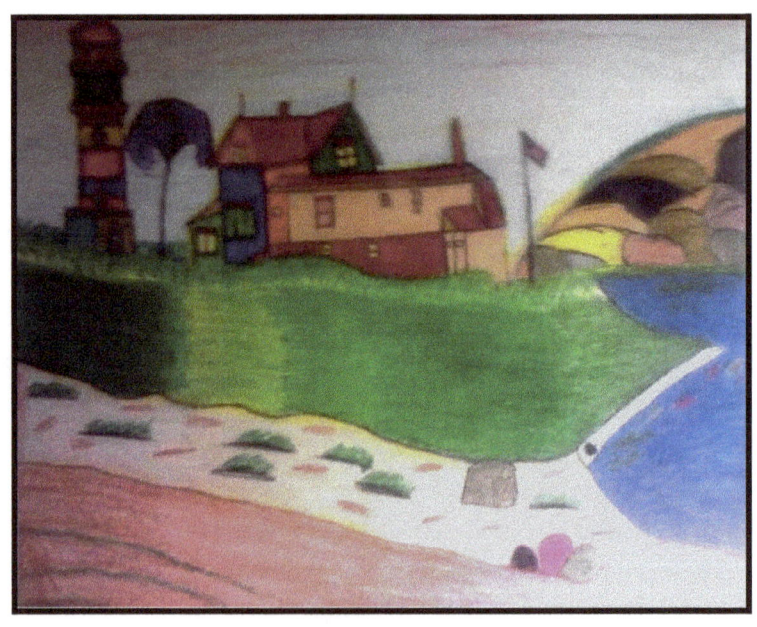

Created By Carolyn Faye Uzzell
56.

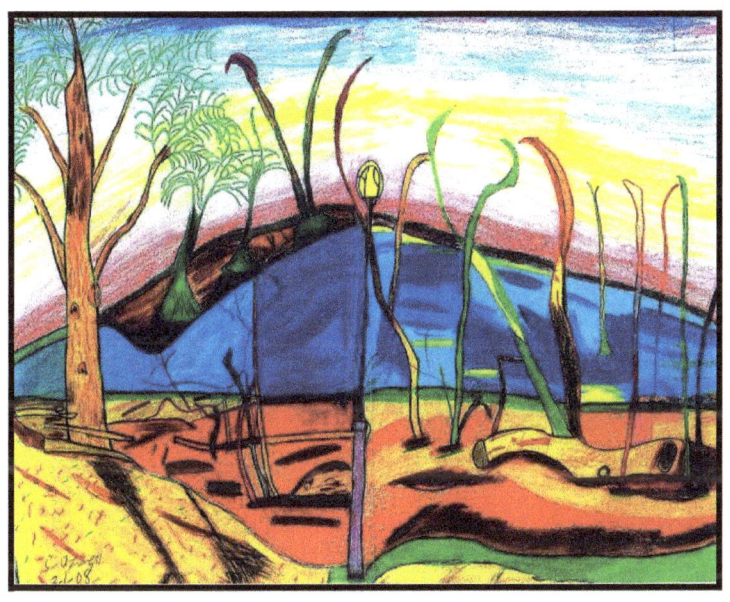

Created By Carolyn Faye Uzzell
57.

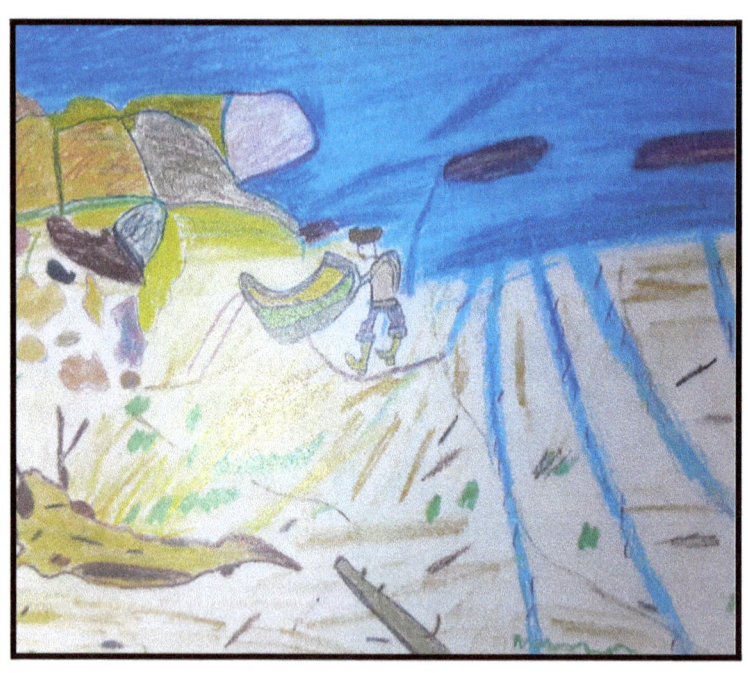

Created By Carolyn Faye Uzzell
58.

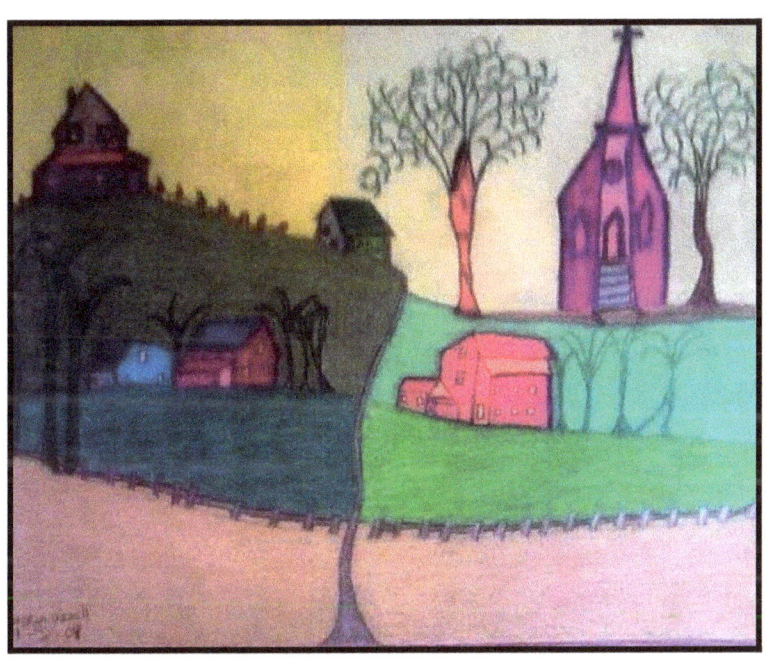

Created By Carolyn Faye Uzzell
59.

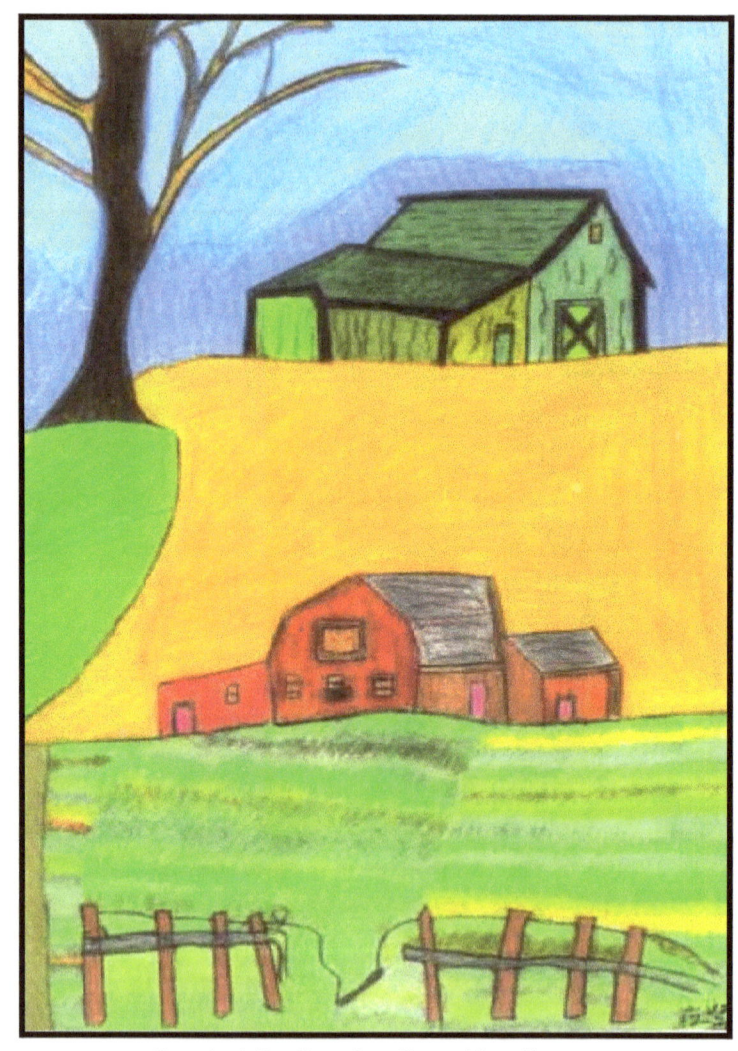

Created By Carolyn Faye Uzzell
60.

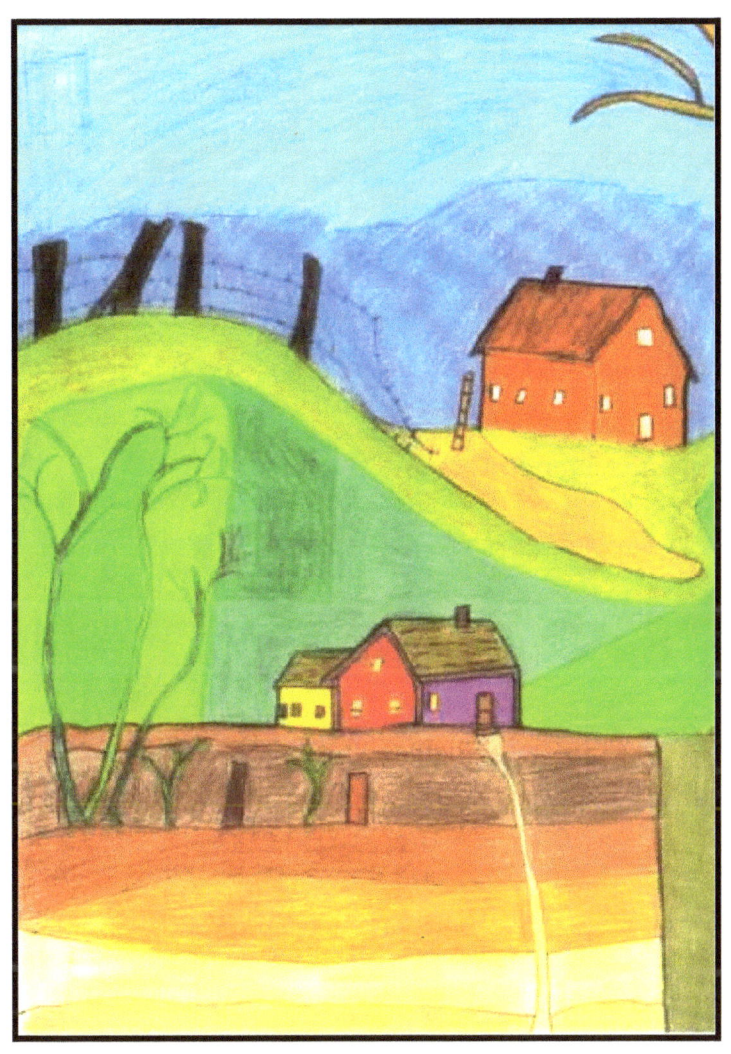

Created By Carolyn Faye Uzzell
61.

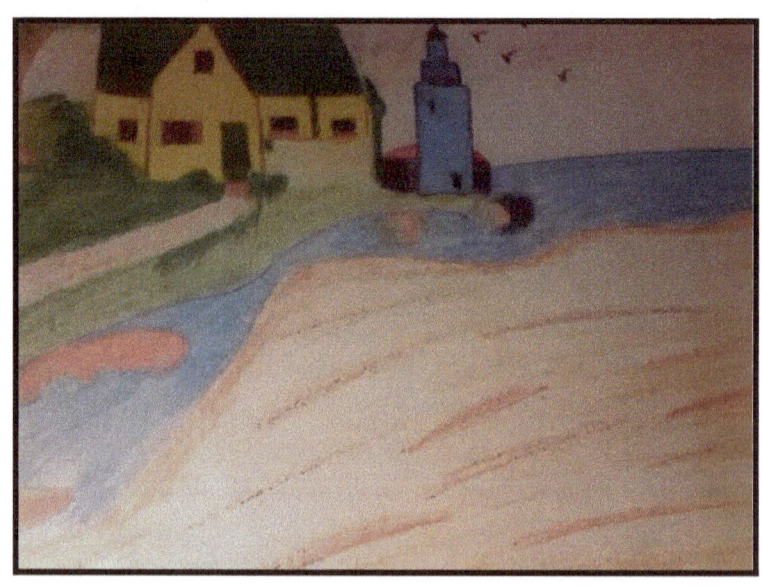

Created By Carolyn Faye Uzzell
62.

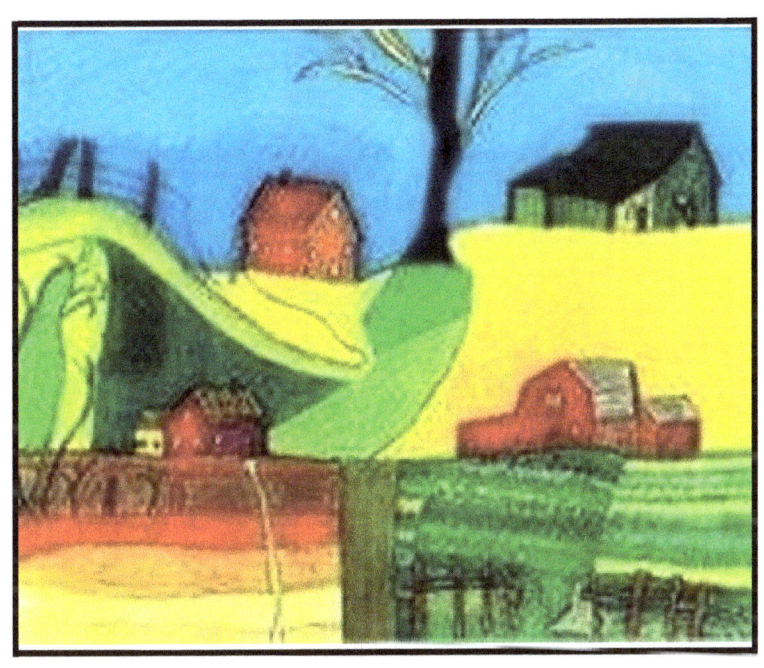

Created By Carolyn Faye Uzzell
63.

~Colorful Blend & Patterns Collection ~

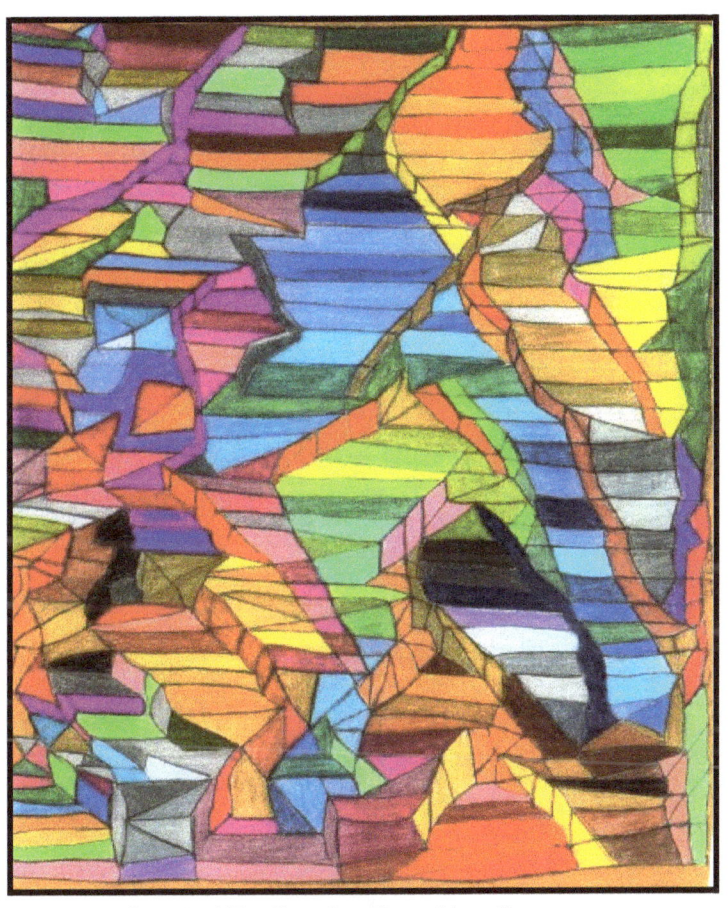

Created By Carolyn Faye Uzzell
64.

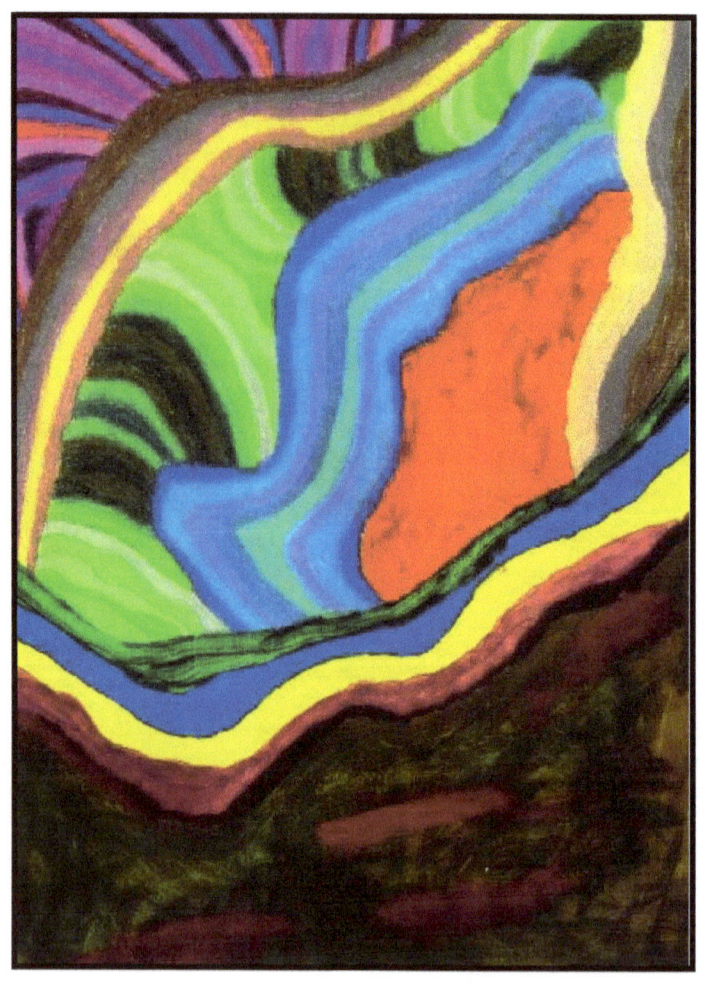

Created By Carolyn Faye Uzzell
65.

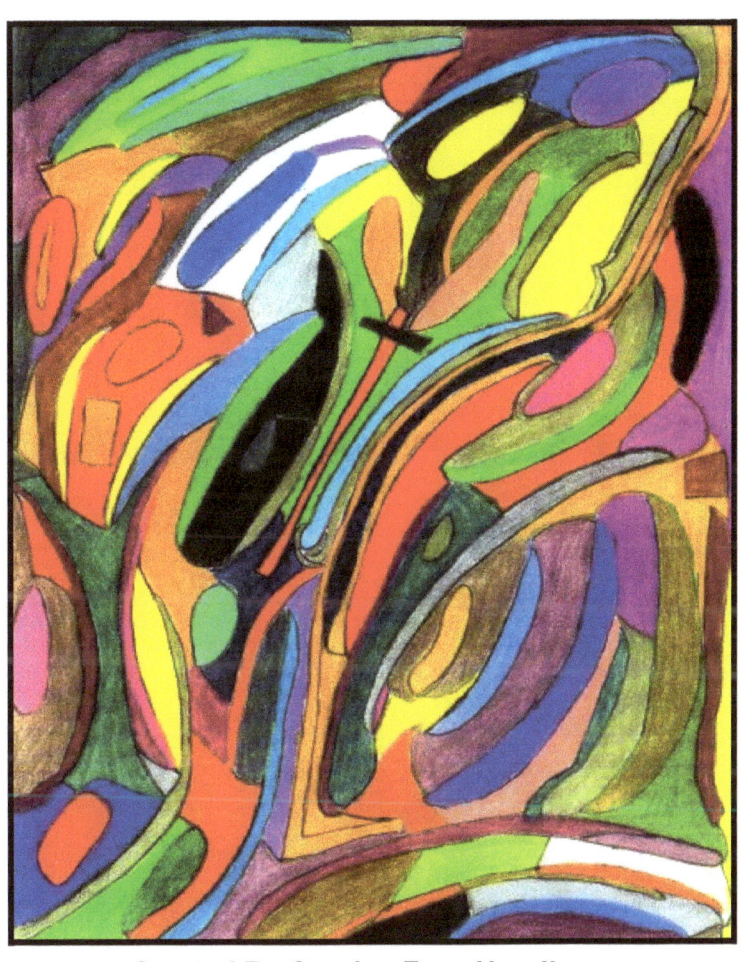

Created By Carolyn Faye Uzzell
66.

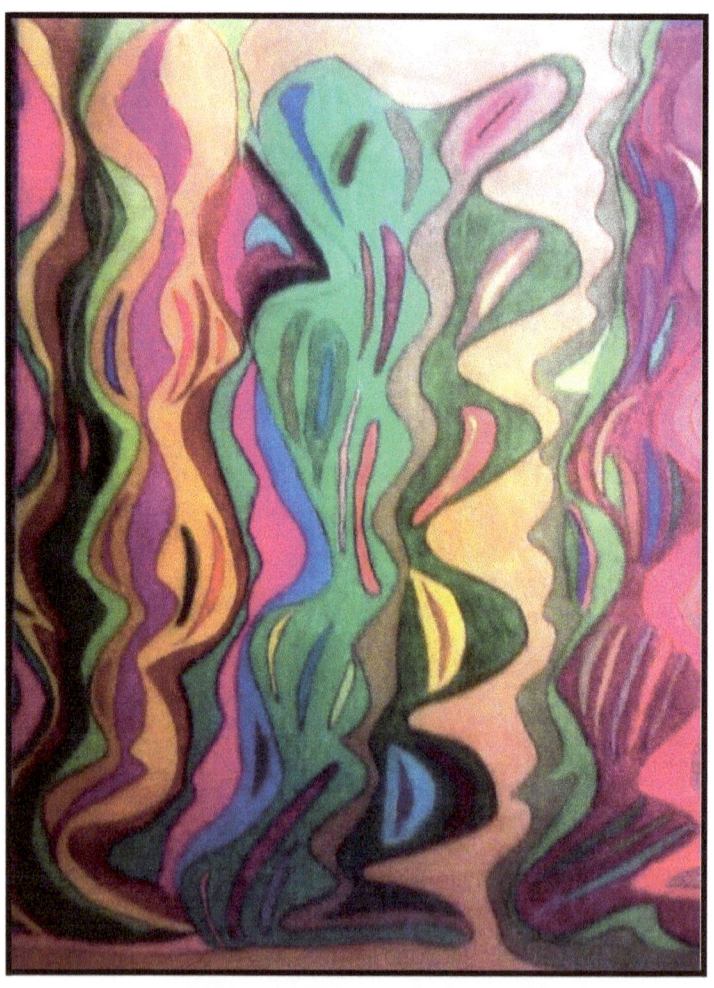

Created By Carolyn Faye Uzzell
67.

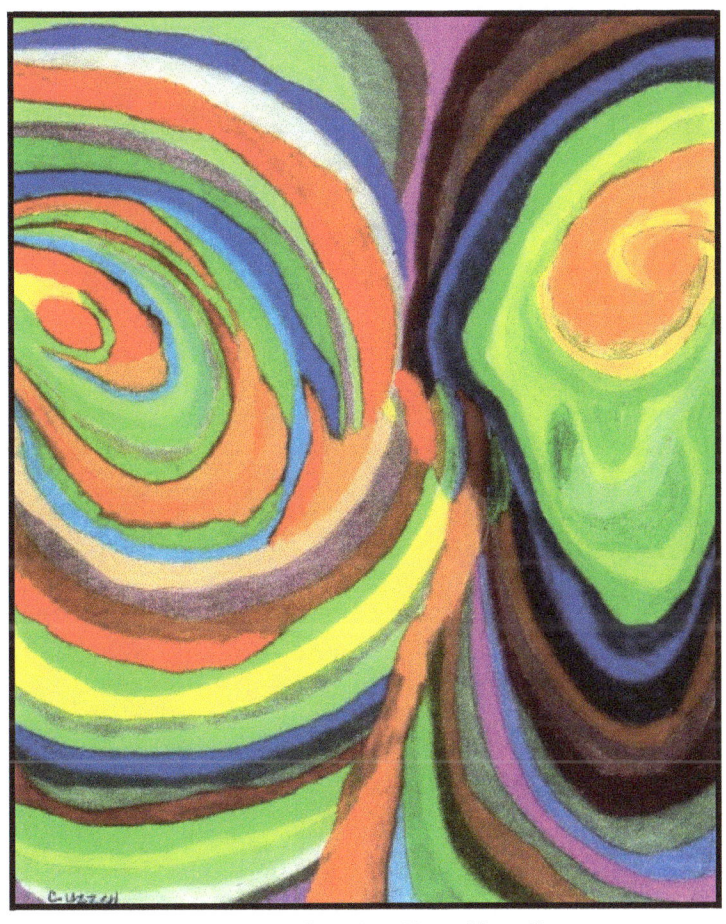

Created By Carolyn Faye Uzzell
68.

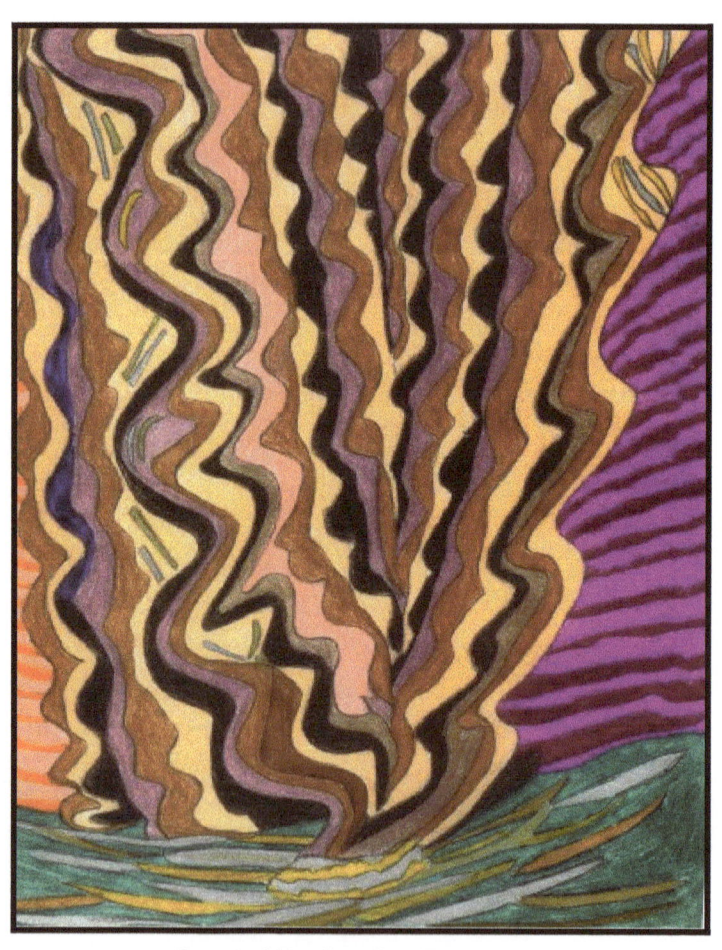

Created By Carolyn Faye Uzzell
69.

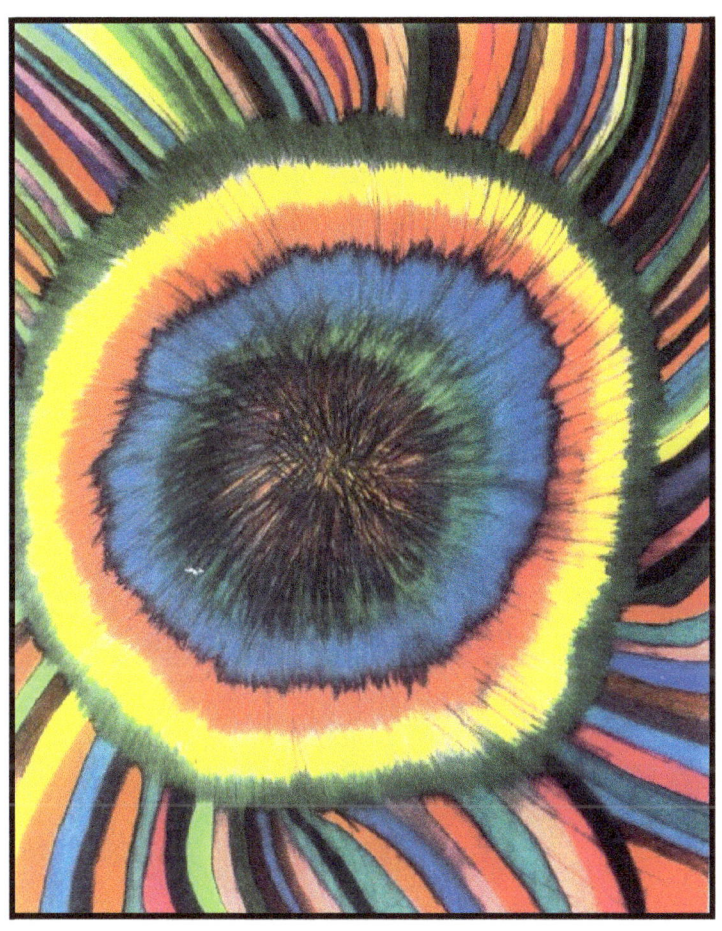

Created By Carolyn Faye Uzell
70.

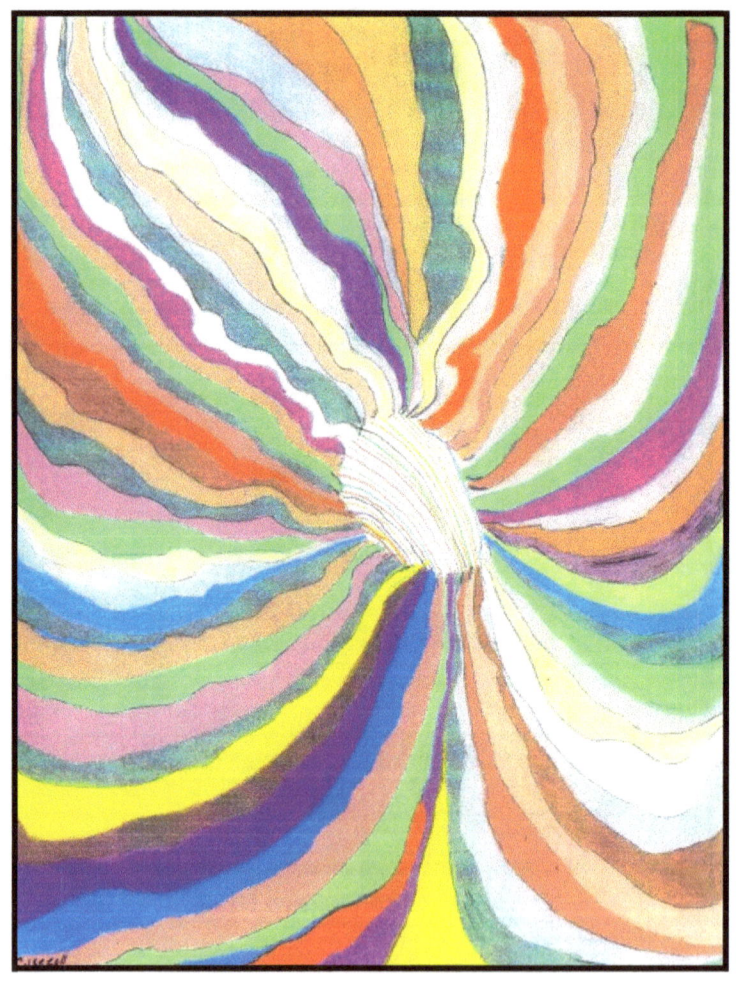

Created By Carolyn Faye Uzzell
71.

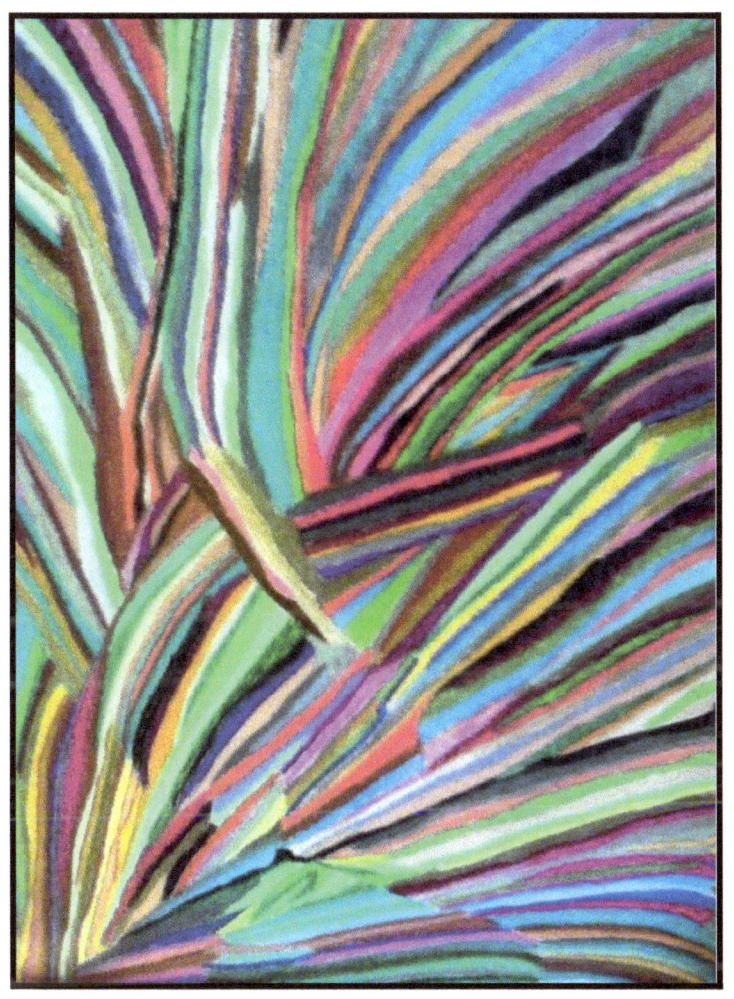

Created By Carolyn Faye Uzzell
72.

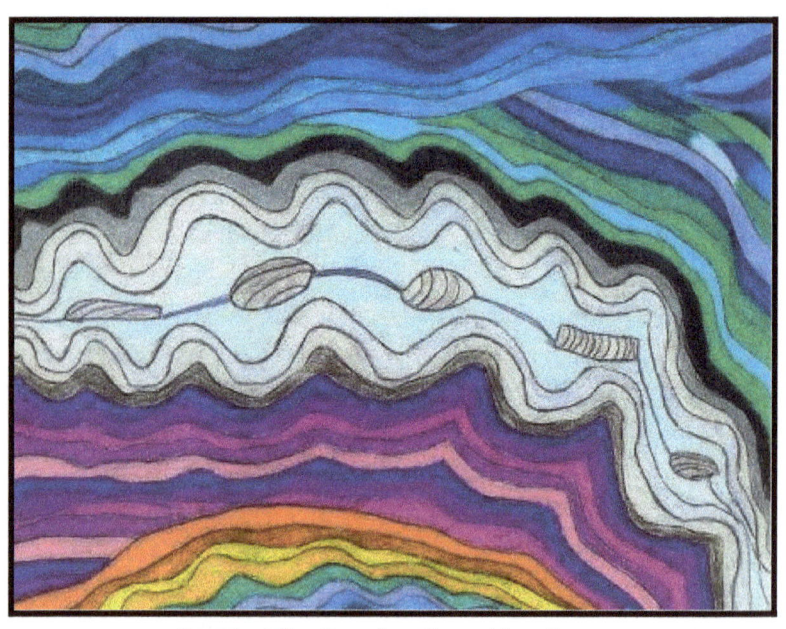

Created By Carolyn Faye Uzzell
73.

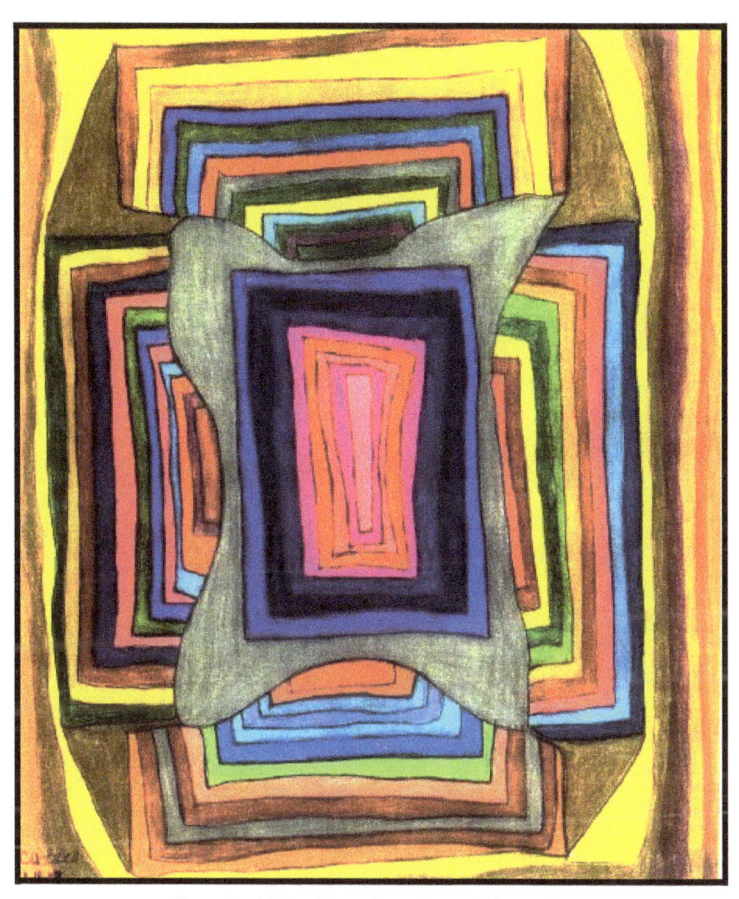

Created By Carolyn Faye Uzzell
74.

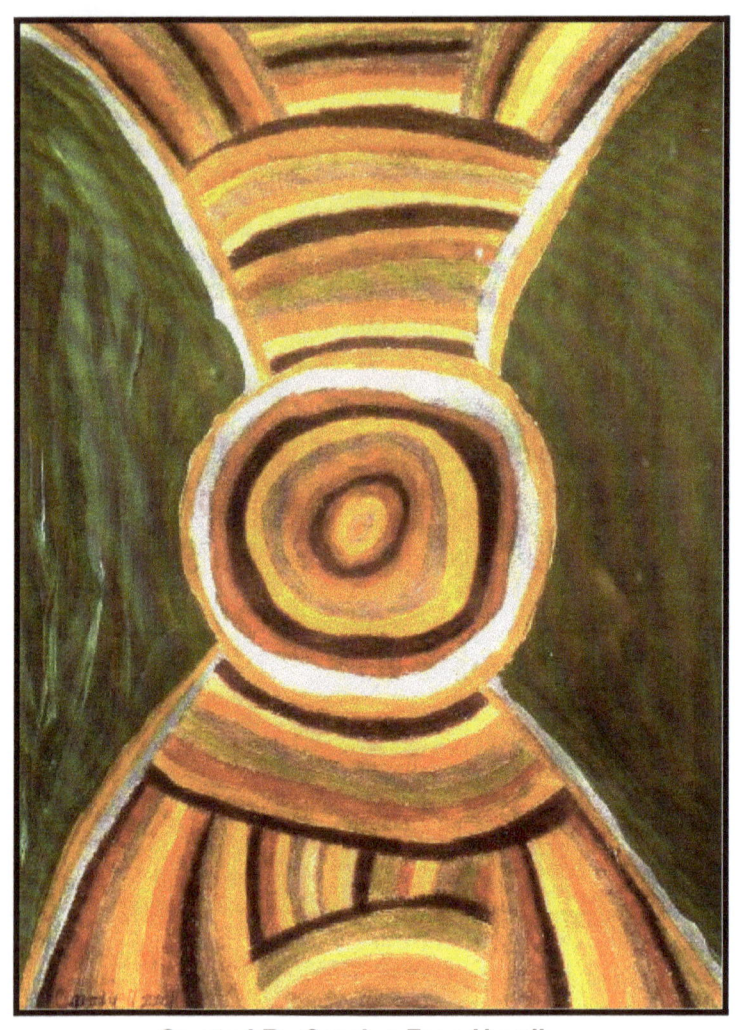

Created By Carolyn Faye Uzzell
75.

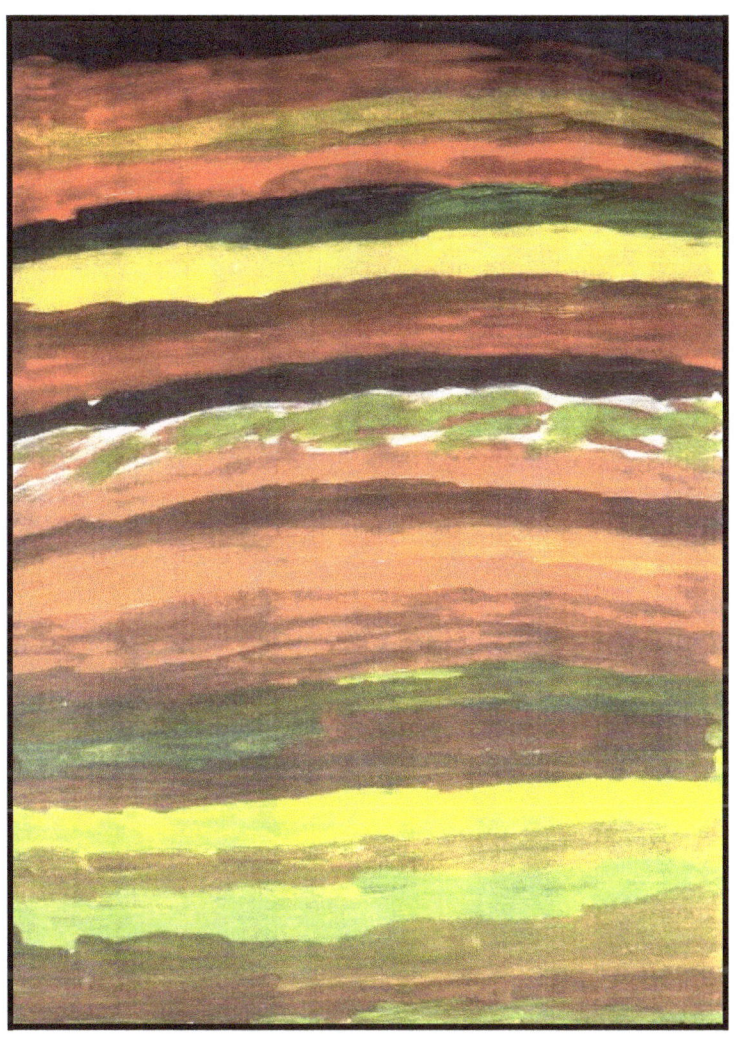

Created By Carolyn Faye Uzzell
76.

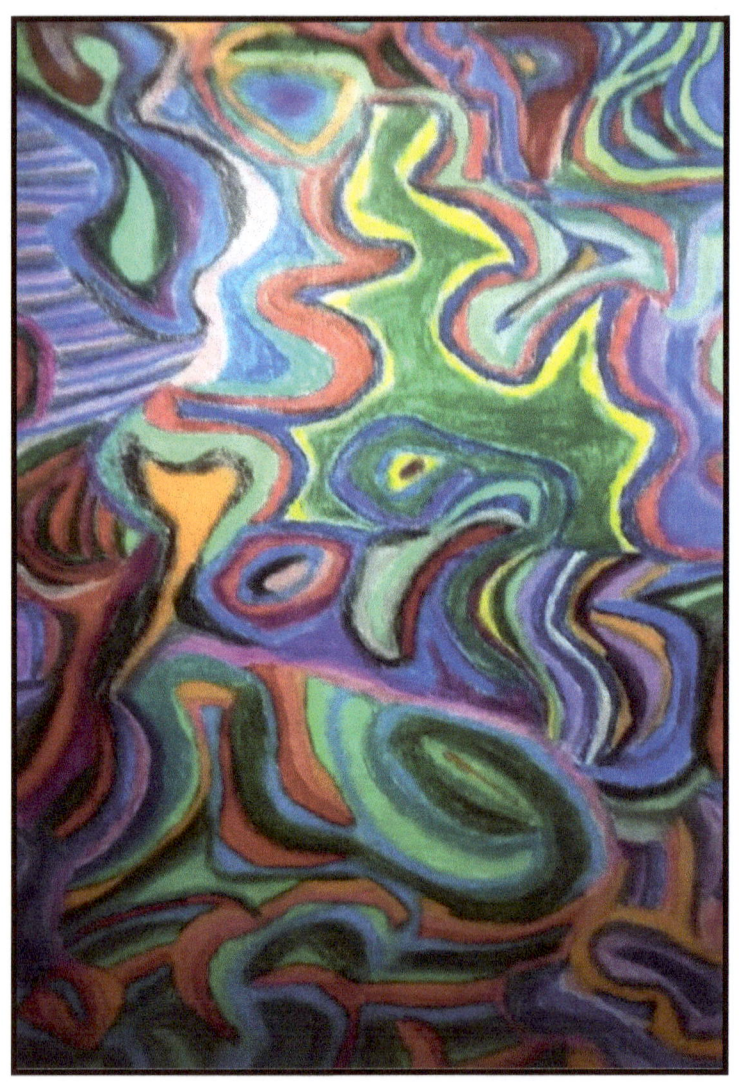

Created By Carolyn Faye Uzzell
77.

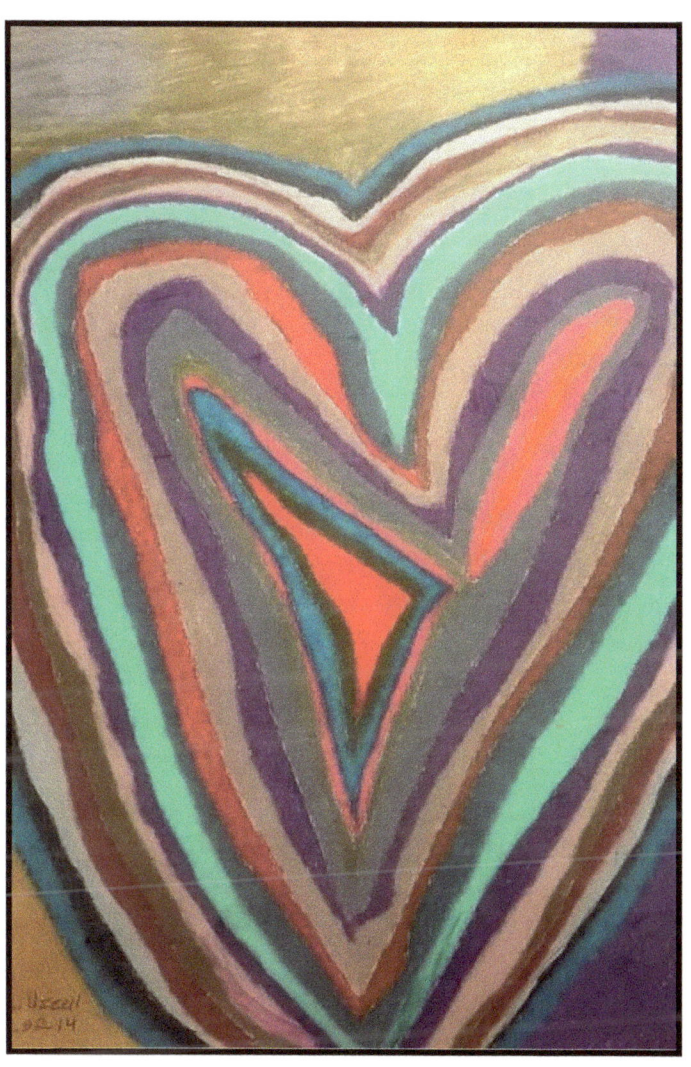

Created By Carolyn Faye Uzzell
78.

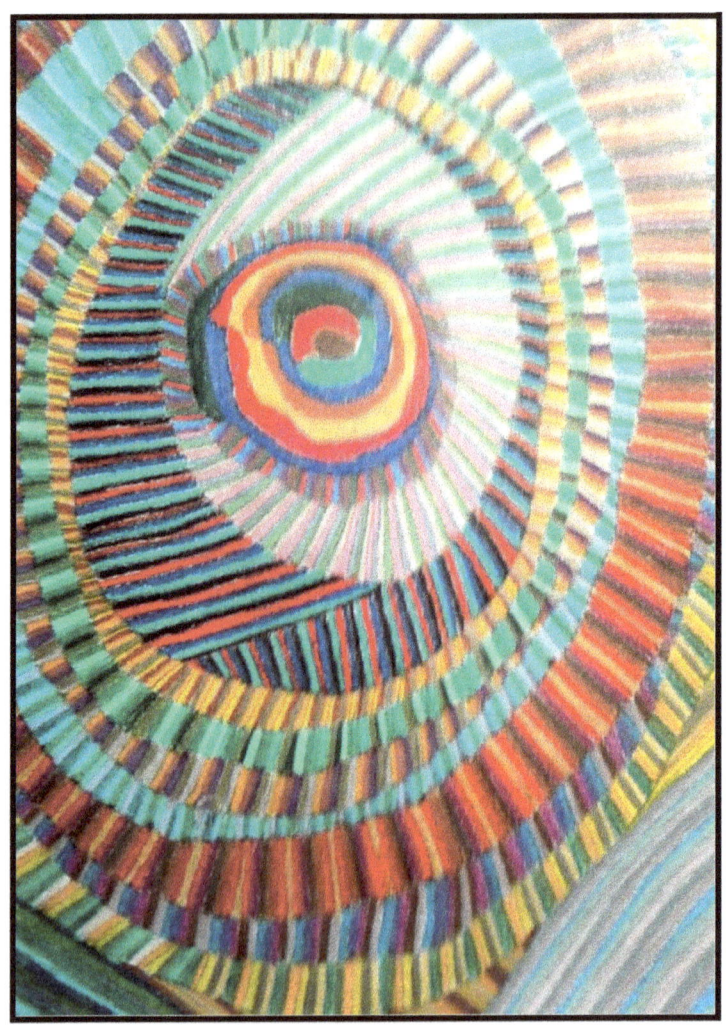

Created By Carolyn Faye Uzzell

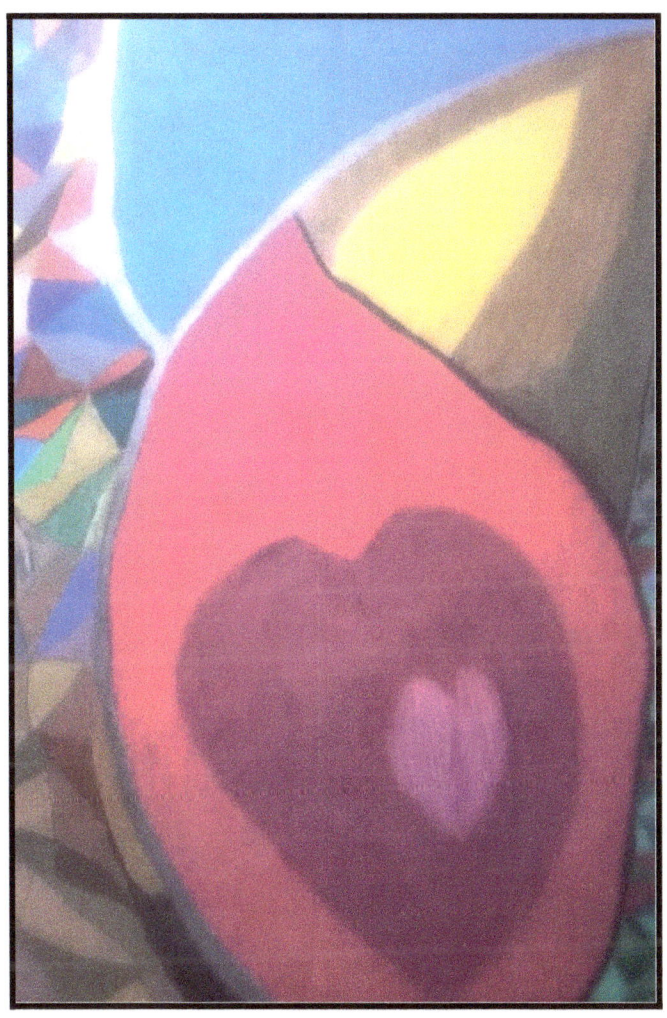

Created By Carolyn Faye Uzzell
80.

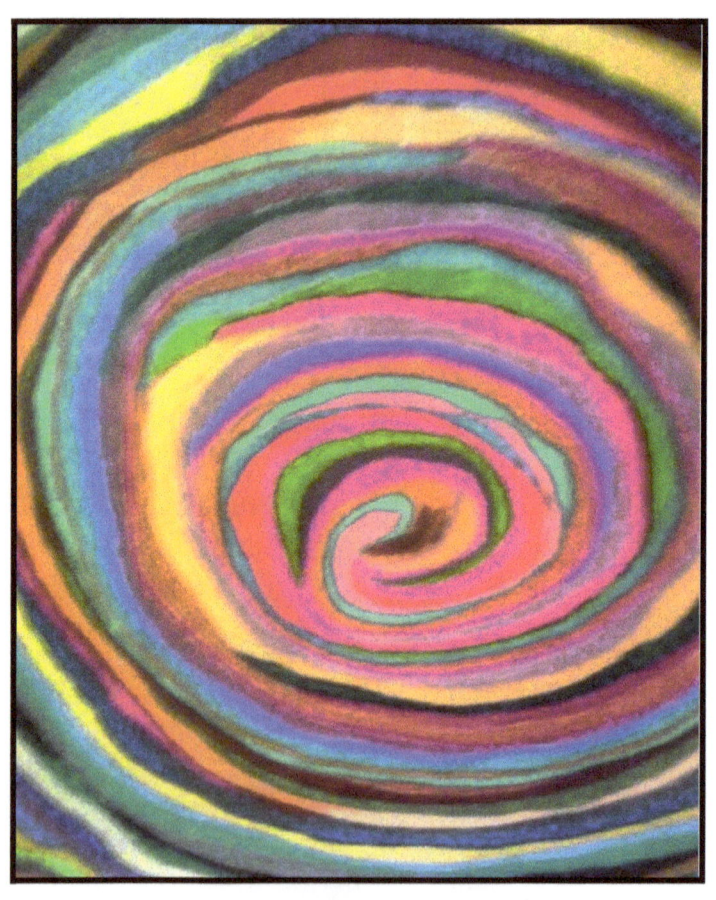

Created By Carolyn Faye Uzzell
81.

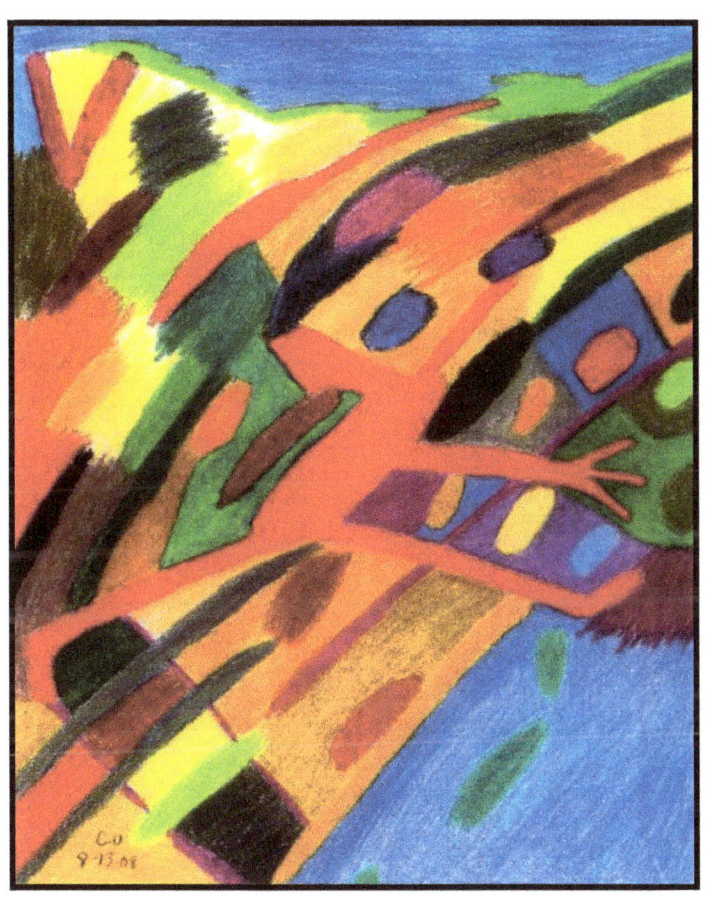

Created By Carolyn Faye Uzzell
82.

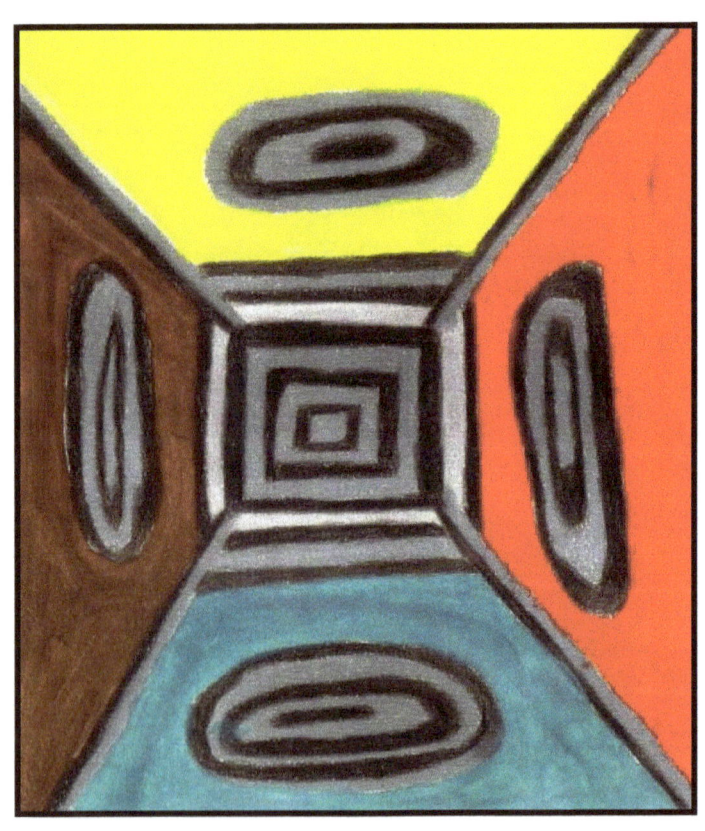

Created By Carolyn Faye Uzzell
83.

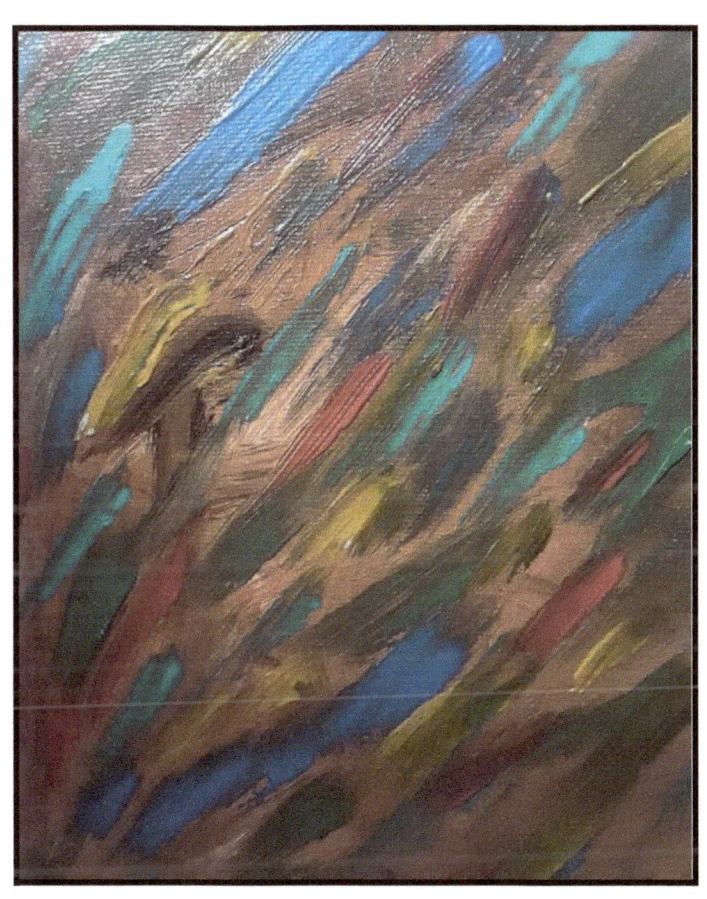

Created By Carolyn Faye Uzzell
84.

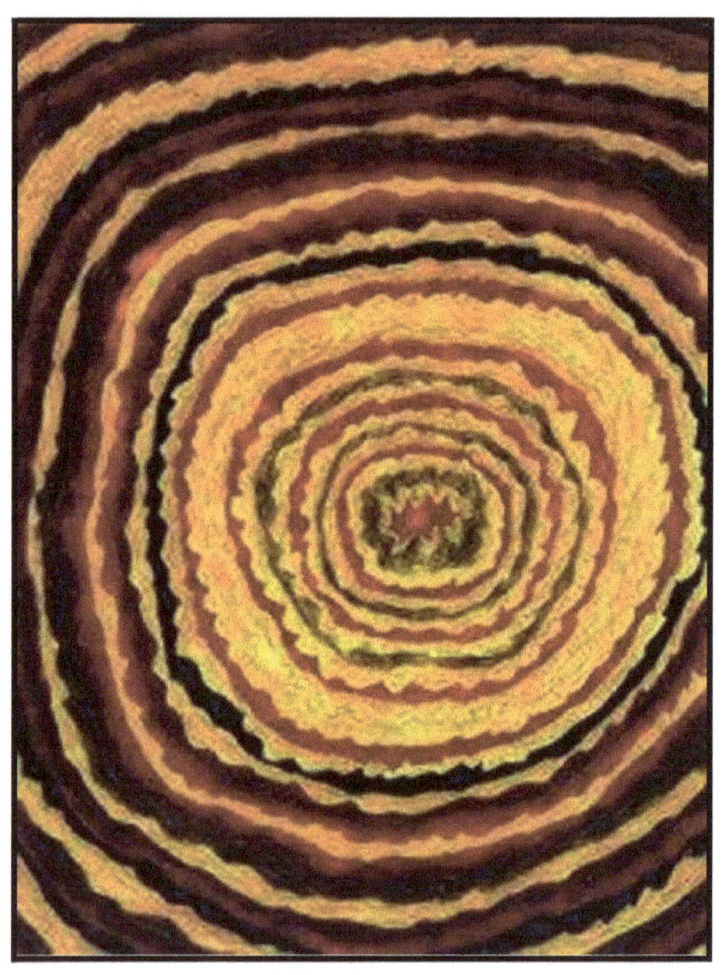

Created By Carolyn Faye Uzzell
85.

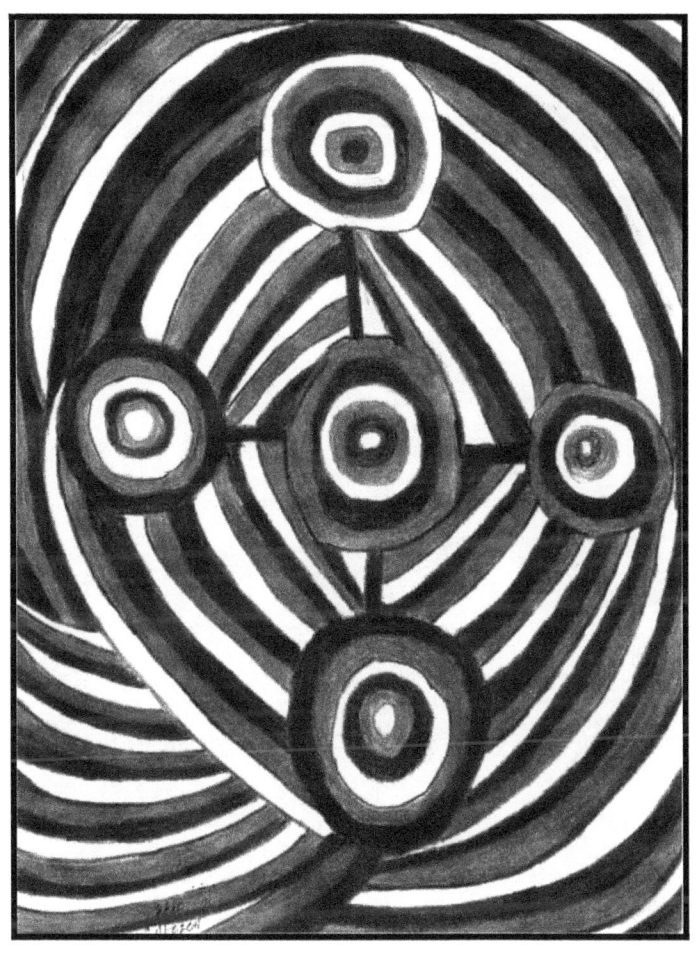

Created By Carolyn Faye Uzzell
86.

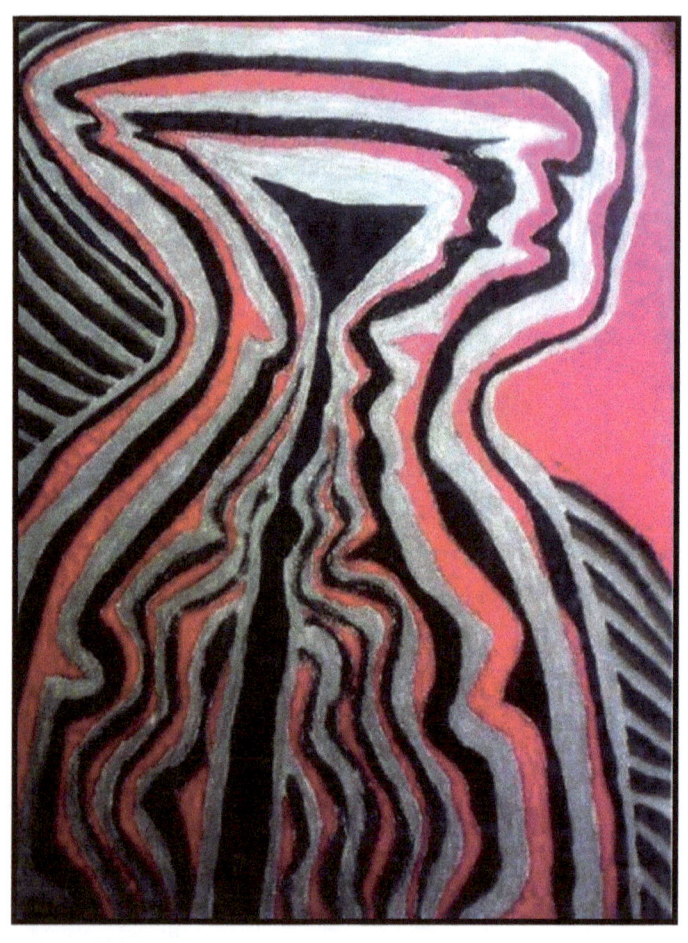

Created By Carolyn Faye Uzzell
87.

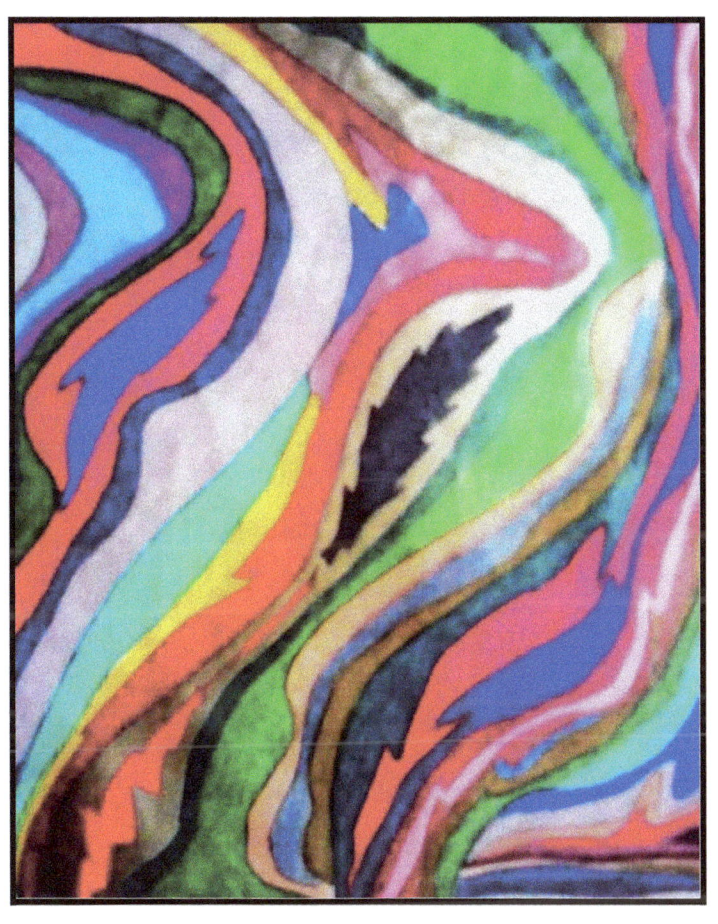

Created By Carolyn Faye Uzzell
88.

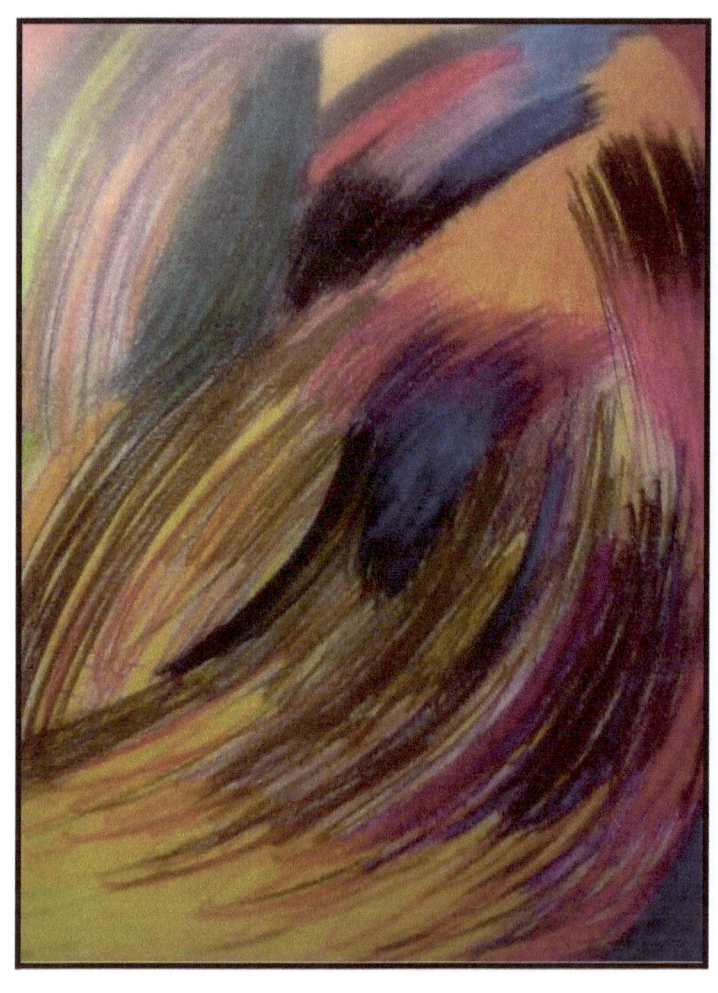

Created By Carolyn Faye Uzzell
89.

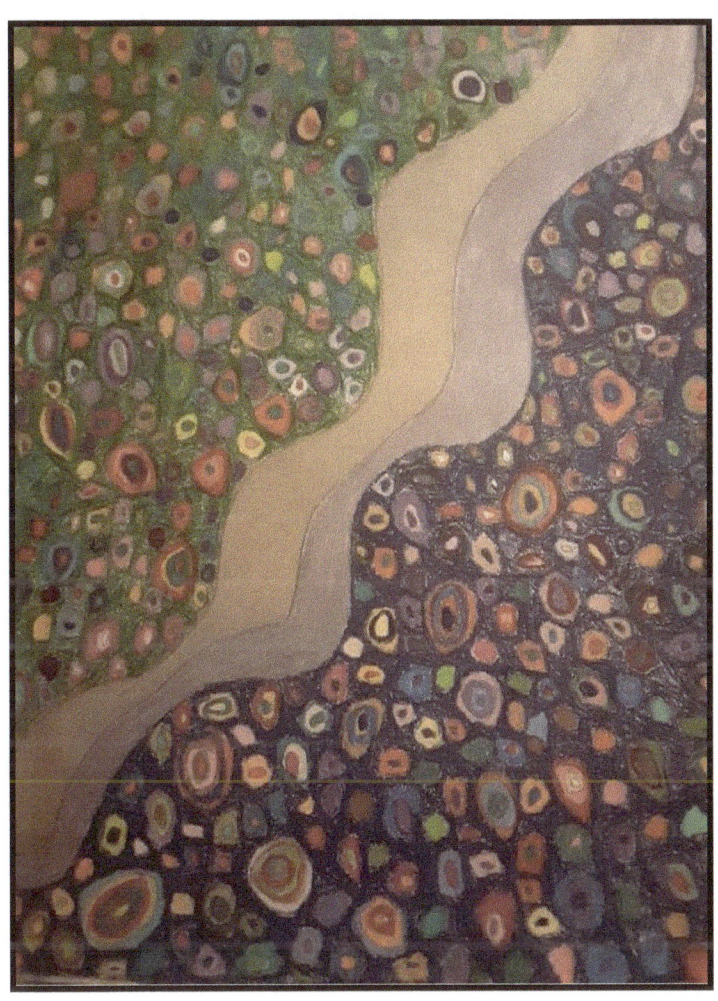

Created By Carolyn Faye Uzzell
90.

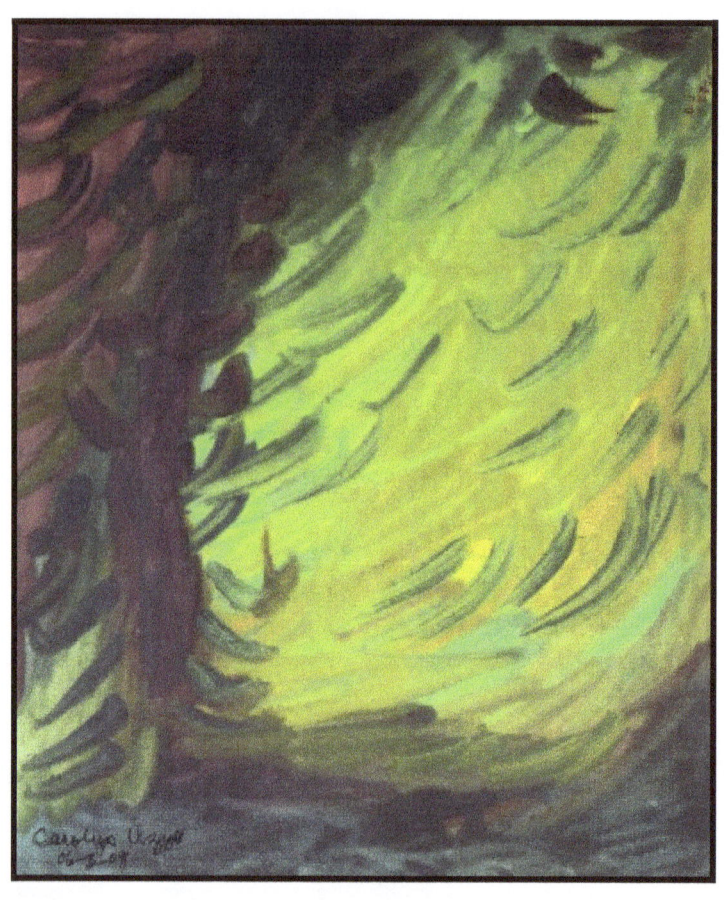

Created By Carolyn Faye Uzzell
91.

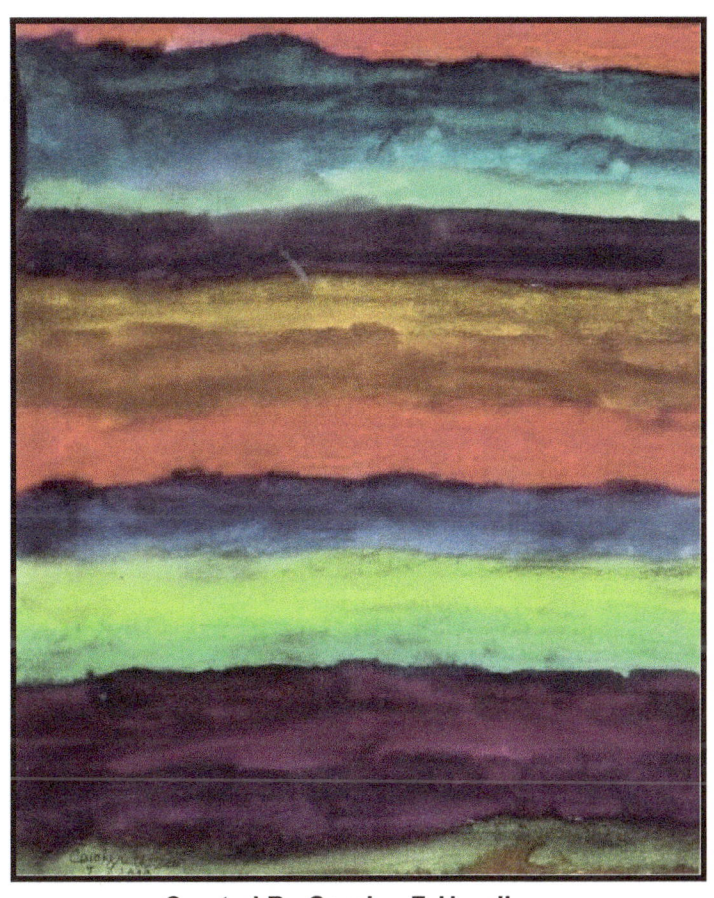

Created By Carolyn F. Uzzell
92.

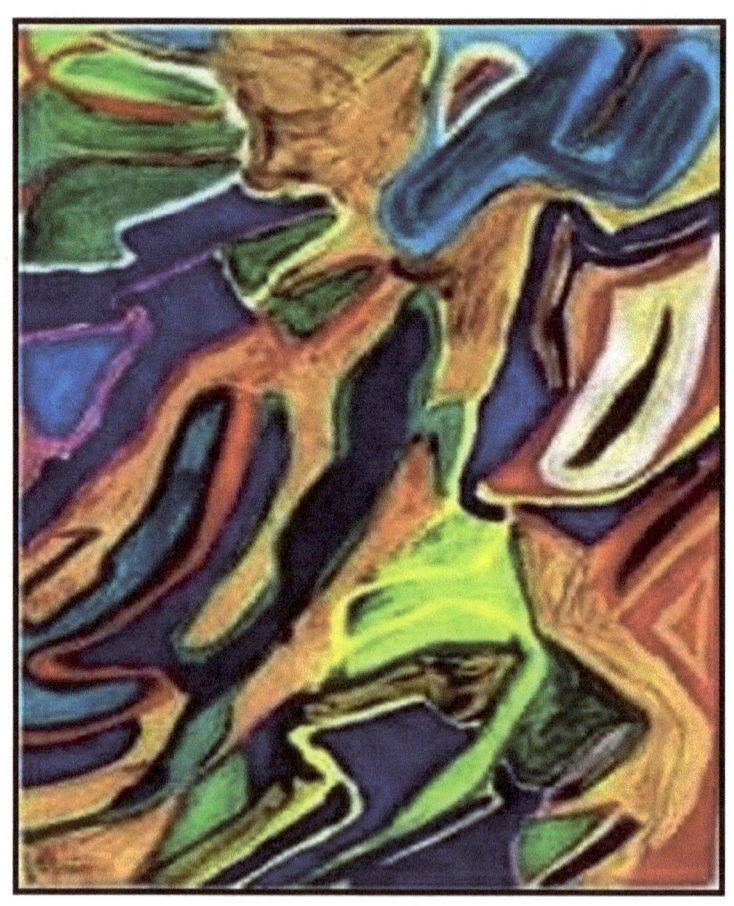

Created By Carolyn Faye Uzzell

Artist

Carolyn Faye Uzzell

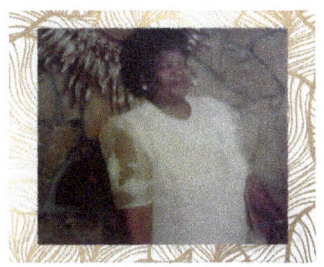

Caroyln F. Uzzell Born in North Carolina relocated to New York. She is inspired by various Art and enjoys expressing her thoughts and emotions by Drawing and Creating beautiful pieces that touch the souls of many admires.

She began this endeavor a few years ago and she continues to fulfill her dream and it is Godly motivated and inspired. These are just a few collections from her many art pieces. She hopes to inspire others to seek their passion as she has found hers.

Carolyn is constantly challenging others to Live for the Lord and share their gifts that God lent to us. She is joyful and positive and this can be seen from her vibrant colors which represent her soul. Her prayer is that God will continue to give her the strength to pursue her passion that will be shared with!

Artist Carolyn Faye Uzzell

~Follow Facebook Page ~

Art For The Soul by Carolyn F Uzzell

https://www.facebook.com/groups/225492487798/

Email Address

carolynuzzell47@aol.com